HAVE YOU CONSIDERED
MY SERVANT?

HAVE YOU CONSIDERED MY SERVANT?

WHEN YOU FEEL LIKE JOB

JAYLONNA STEVETTE

J MERRILL

J Merrill Publishing, Inc.
434 Hillpine Drive
Columbus, OH 43207
www.JMerrill.pub

Library of Congress Control Number: 2024909372
ISBN-13: 978-1-961475-31-1 (Paperback)
ISBN-13: 978-1-961475-32-8 (eBook)

Book Title: Have You Considered My Servant?: When You Feel Like Job
Author: Jaylonna Stevette

CONTENTS

I DON'T IDENTIFY AS A CHRISTIAN

Let me start this book by saying that I don't claim to be a Christian. I know that will shock and turn off many from this book, but that's the truth of the matter. I am not a Christian. Let me clarify some things before you take your rocks out to stone me. I have a strong Christian background and have been part of one of the biggest ministries in the city I have lived in for a long time. I was a faithful church member, married into the ministry, and even held leadership for years, so I know who Christ is. I just don't identify with the everyday goings-on—church, ministry, and the pomp and circumstance of what has become religious acts. I have a Christ consciousness, but I don't subscribe to any one religion or practice because I have found in my own journey that all things can be useful. So, if you're looking for this book to confirm your own religion, this book is not for you.

This book is designed to take you on a powerful journey of understanding your own trials and how they relate to your relationship with God. Whether you say God, Source, or infinite intelligence, it all points back to the source of it all, the source of our being, to whom we are connected. I don't believe God is either man or woman; I believe even the word God is too small to describe creation. There may be times I use scripture references to appeal to my point, and of course, since I'm taking you on Job's journey, God will be referenced many times in this book. For the sake of the book and the narrator of the chapter, I will also reference God as "He" at times as well. But again, what I have come to know God to be, there is no description that can really pinpoint what God is.

What is this book about? Job and YOU. Believe it or not, no matter where you are in your journey that you call life, you are a lot like Job, and as you begin to see that, hopefully, it will be eye-opening for you to know that everything you go through has a purpose behind it.

Sometimes, we ask ourselves why we go through the things we do. Sometimes, we ask ourselves why God doesn't stop certain things from happening to us, why we don't have what we want, and many other questions. The funny thing is, we don't begin to ask these questions until we find ourselves in a place of discontent. Some of you don't even talk to God until all hell breaks loose, but I won't go there. But God knows.

I also didn't decide or choose to write this book. I was chosen to write it for whatever reason God saw fit. As a church member, I was familiar with the story of Job. Still, God shed light on Job's story through my own experiences, which were so enlightening that the world needs to know. As we go on this journey together, may the revelation of your own experiences draw you closer to the one who created you.

1

WHO WAS JOB REALLY?

Have you ever been asked the question, "Who are you?" The question itself is a loaded one, and if you really want the honest answer, it's something you would have to think about and process to get the true answer. Who are you, really? The bigger question could also be, whoever you think you are, does it align with what others think of you? Your perception of yourself and what others think about who you are could be two completely opposite perceptions. A person can see the obvious things about you, such as being a parent, spouse, or nationality, but knowing who you truly are goes deeper than that. It's the same with Job. We know surface things about him, but what do we really know?

According to the Bible, Job was a man who lived in the land of Uz. He had ten children, a wife, and great substance. The Bible also indicates that he was a man who loved God. Let's dive right into Chapter 1, shall we?

1 There was a man in the land of Uz, whose name

> *was Job; and that man was perfect and*
> *upright, and one that feared God, and*
> *eschewed evil.*
>
> 2 *And there were born unto him seven sons and*
> *three daughters.*
>
> 3 *His substance also was seven thousand sheep,*
> *and three thousand camels, and five hundred*
> *yoke of oxen, and five hundred she-asses, and*
> *a very great household; so that this man was*
> *the greatest of all the men of the east.*

This text definitely says a lot. Job was referenced as perfect, upright, and God-fearing—who can compete with that? I don't know about you, but my impression of Job from just this text alone always told me I had a long way to go to be who I was called to be. Perfect? Geesh! The text also tells me that Job was a man of notoriety. Being referenced as the greatest of all the men of the east is no small gesture. According to the Bible—God-inspired—this is who Job was, and nothing else was added to that text. Everything else about Job is inferred; our assumptions of what and who we believe Job is. What about his wife and his children? What kind of father and husband was he? Was he a shrewd businessman, or no? To have thousands of livestock and lands and a great household with servants, the man had to be doing something right. But nobody is perfect, right? It gets confusing because the scripture says he was a perfect man. But God's perfection and man's perfection are not the same.

As a former Christian, I also looked at the story of Job like this: Poor Job, he was perfect, and the devil just came in and messed with him for no reason at all. He lost it all. Why, God? I made assumptions just like everyone else, and since the good book gives us nothing else, we can only assume. And on that note, since we're assuming, I'll share my own enlightenment. Like everyone else, Job probably struggled with parenting, marriage, and managing his friendships. He probably feared how he was perceived in the eyes of others and had to stay a couple of steps ahead in many areas to ensure that things in his world ran smoothly.

We also know Job had ten children. Anyone who is a parent knows that each child is different. You can instill the same principles of life in each child, and the outcome will be different for each child because they are all different. How many of us have grown children whose paths have surprised you? Sometimes, I look at my own kids and wonder if I raised them to think like that. Job had ten kids, so I'm sure he and his wife had many instances where their sanity was questioned. The Bible says Job was perfect, but the same wasn't said about his family; this has always been assumed. As a matter of fact, Job seemed to question the judgment of his grown children in Chapter 1, verse 4:

> *4 And his sons went and feasted in their houses,*
> *every one his day; and sent and called for*
> *their three sisters to eat and to drink with*
> *them.*
> *5 And it was so, when the days of their feasting*
> *were gone about, that Job sent and sanctified*
> *them, and rose up early in the morning, and*
> *offered burnt offerings according to the*
> *number of them all: for Job said, It may be*
> *that my sons have sinned, and cursed God in*
> *their hearts. Thus did Job continually.*

The last words, "Thus did Job continually." Why? Why would this man who was so perfect before God be so consumed with the activities of his grown children? Because he knew what all parents know, our children can be one way with us and wild and crazy when we are not around! Now, I'm not saying that was the case. But, if Job had to continually offer burnt offerings, he definitely had fears about his legacy and what it would become. Notice his burnt offerings were for ALL his children. I'm no rocket scientist, but I know the Bible enough to know that simple prayer and burnt offerings differ. Burnt offerings in the Bible are meant for the atoning of sin. Job was so afraid whatever they were into would need to be atoned for. To me, that's very telling. When you look at Job from a human perspective, you begin to see that he dealt with many things that we deal with today, yet he was still considered perfect. That alone should give you hope, especially if you parent unruly children. You're not alone.

What about Job as a husband, as a friend? We will dive deeper into that as we progress, but all I'm saying again is that God's perfection and ours are not the same. People always say to look at who you're connected to because it may indicate who you may also be. Is there truth to that? Absolutely! Crackheads and millionaires don't mingle together. Does that make sense? Job's stature in life tells us he was favored, but his relationships, as you will see, will reflect his humanity.

Who are *you* in relationship to Job?

Now that I have given you a small glimpse of who Job was, the very next question points back to you: Who are you in relationship to Job? If you're reading this book, something about it obviously piqued your interest. Some of you may be familiar with Job and can relate to how he felt, and you are looking for some answers. Others may not know the story or wonder how this book can help you. And others may have received this book by recommendation. In any of those circumstances, you're probably on the edge of your seat trying to figure out what I will say next. The truth is very simple: if you only grasp it, no matter where you are in your "trial," you will find peace. If you've been through a Job experience, what I say next will confirm this truth: God chose *you*. That's it. You were chosen. It sounds so mystical, but it truly is a peaceful truth. Just walk with me through this book, and I promise by the end, you'll understand more why one or more sequences of your life seem so hard that you felt like dying. But if you're still living, you also see the beauty of understanding the why and the lessons behind your Job experience. And since we are all unique individuals, our trials, experiences, and lessons will be uniquely tailored to us in life's journey.

Some of you wonder, "Who is she, and what makes her qualified to even touch on this subject?" Especially those who know me or have followed my social media presence for some time. And I know some of my former churchmates are asking that question for real. I don't claim to be a biblical scholar or have any seminary education. Well, I'll break down what qualifies me with confidence. Then, I'll be brutally transparent about my journey and who I am. Here are the things that qualify me:

I. I am a writer and a good one at that. I have been a writer and creative for as long as I can remember. As a child, I wrote plays for my siblings to act out.

As an adult, I wrote poetry, produced my own stage play that sold out, traveled to one city, and was even accepted into the Atlanta Black Theater Festival. As this book is written, I have three other published books, two audiobooks, and a story-based podcast with a following in sixty-two countries. This book, however, isn't about *my* many successes, and you'll see that shortly.

2. I'm great at listening to instructions and executing clear actions towards my goals. A person who can go within and see the vision, create it, and execute it can *definitely* be used by God. But most of all, I listen to God. I have heard Him clearly all my life, and every time I trust God by listening, it reaffirms that I hear from the source of it all.

3. Simply this. I love God. And God knows I love the Source.

Now that we have my magnificent qualifications out of the way let me tell you who God chose truly for this book and this experience. I am a fifty-two-year-old woman who shows her half-naked body on social media. I write erotica. Hell, I even have an OnlyFans page—imagine that. My podcast with this big audience is called *Naughty Tales*, so you know it's more naughty than nice. I have been called many things since I started writing erotica. I have been called a whore and a backslider. When I opened myself up to practicing spirituality by adding meditation, affirmations, sage, and crystals, I was labeled a witch. I also know what it feels like to be judged and talked about by friends, family, co-workers, and such. But that did not stop me from doing what I felt I was called to do. If your mouth is open in shock, I need you to close it because, at first, I was just as surprised as you when God came in like a PSA and disrupted my day-to-day but also provided me grace in all of this. I don't want to get ahead of myself, but you will see.

If what I just mentioned has shocked you to the core and you can't wrap your mind around how God can use me to shed light on the story of Job, well, He definitely has a track record for these things. Does the Bible not say that God uses the foolish things of this world to confound the wise? This means God can use whoever He wants to accomplish the greater good. God is *the* Source. God is infinite intelligence. If that is not enough proof for you, in Numbers 22, God used a donkey to speak:

> 28 *And the Lord opened the mouth of the ass, and she said unto Balaam: 'What have I done unto thee, that thou hast smitten me these three times?'*

What was going on so horribly that God could not use a human to accomplish what was needed? Or perhaps what needed to be communicated was so detrimental that God had to use an ass to get His point across. If God wants something to get done, it will, period. But not by a whore, you're probably thinking, right? She writes erotica; how could God *possibly* be in agreement with that? Well, I'll end the Chapter this way; remember Hosea? Didn't he marry a whore named Gomer because God told him to:

> 2 *The beginning of the word of the Lord by Hosea. And the Lord said to Hosea, "Go, take unto thee a wife of whoredoms and children*

of whoredoms: for the land hath committed
great whoredom, departing from the Lord."

There you have it. In actuality, Gomer was not a prostitute.
She wasn't getting paid as the lady of the hour. Hosea did
not go into a whorehouse and pick her up, carrying her
away like the ending of the movie *An Officer and a Gentleman*.
Her homegirls did not cheer her on as they walked into the
sunset. Gomer was very promiscuous and had a lot of extra-
marital affairs. I've proven my point, but I really didn't need
to. But as readers, I needed you to understand that it doesn't
matter who you are. God can use you. Writing this book
doesn't make me better or worse than anyone else. I'm
simply completing the task at hand. So now that all of the
pleasantries are out of the way, let's take Job's journey
together.

2

WHEN YOUR NAME IS IN THEIR MOUTH

Now that you know who you are in relation to Job and the fact that you are chosen, let's talk about *why* this happens. Someone is talking about *you* and since God has chosen you for the task, there is a clear conversation about you and what *you* are made of. There is always someone thinking about you—good or bad—and if you're in *my* line of work or anything edgy, your name will come across someone's mouth in conversation. There will be doubters in your life when you want to do something great, and those kinds of people will forever be talking.

In the days of Job, his biggest hater was obviously Satan. Let's look at Chapter 1, verses 6-8:

> *6 Now there was a day when the sons of God*
> *came to present themselves before the Lord,*
> *and Satan came also among them.*
> *7 And the Lord said unto Satan, "Whence comest*
> *thou?" Then Satan answered the Lord, and*

> said, "From going to and fro in the earth, and
> from walking up and down in it."
> 8 And the Lord said unto Satan, "Hast thou
> considered my servant Job, that there is none
> like him in the earth, a perfect and an upright
> man, one that feareth God, and escheweth
> evil?"

Ok, let's break this down a bit. Verse 6 says the sons of men came before God, and Satan was there too. Why was Satan there? Notice he said Satan and not Lucifer. Lucifer is the bright and morning star, his beloved. Satan is not. But that is another teaching I am exploring, so I won't get into it. Again, Satan was not supposed to be there, but yet there he was. Then he had the audacity to say he was *looking* for someone to make a fool of God. To God's face. Bold.

That's how the little satans in our lives are. The lowercase satans are usually in places they shouldn't be, talking about what you are doing, what you're not doing, and what *they think* you should be doing. Always got your name in their mouths. But God always has another conversation about you. Notice the nature of God will never be outdone, so he says, "Have you considered my servant Job?" Not only that, but he brags about him and how upright he is. See the balance there? God will also send those to you who speak highly of you and root for you in life. People who will have your name in their mouth in a positive way. Putting respect on your name.

When God puts those types of people in your life, don't think that Satan will bow down; he and his haters always have an answer; look at verses 9-11:

9 *Then Satan answered the Lord, and said, "Doth Job fear God for nought?*

10 *Hast not thou made an hedge about him, and about his house, and about all that he hath on every side? thou hast blessed the work of his hands, and his substance is increased in the land.*

11 *But put forth thine hand now, and touch all that he hath, and he will curse thee to thy face.*

Wow, Satan. He says that the only reason Job reveres God is because of all his substance. He even challenged Job's loyalty to God. Basically, said if he had nothing, he would curse God to his face. Why was Satan even concerned with Job or anyone else in the first place? Job was minding his business, living his life. Job had no concern about Satan; he was simply doing what great men do, what they are called to.

And so, it is with your haters. Again, they assess what you have and why you have it! Oh, don't have a nice house or drive a nice car; the little satans who have your name in their mouths have a big problem with that. They run around asking your God-given connections how you got those things or make their own assumptions. They assume if you have more than them, it couldn't have been gotten honorably. If you have less than them and you're a rising star, they hate that too. Why try to please these types of people? Because no matter what you say or do, you can't. The truth is, the folks who talk the most about you hold no value to who you are and who you are becoming, and when you realize that, it will be a game changer for your life. Small minds talk about people, as the saying goes.

Like Job on my journey to growing into my being, I had haters along the way. Hell, I still do. My haters have come from past friends, coworkers, and "play" family members. When I use that term, I mean friends so close they are recognized as family. Oh, I don't want to exclude former friends of worship from the list of those who keep my name in their mouths. These are the type of folks that constantly watch you from afar in some way—social media, similar connections, etc. They're always watching and asking others about you, or they happen to hear about or see something you're doing, and it gets them talking again. Take the time to thank those who continually talk about you because they are on their assignment to prove to themselves that you have no worth. It makes them feel better to believe that. So go ahead, let them. I won't directly name them in this book, but they know who they are. I need you to acknowledge that they will be there on your journey, so don't be surprised. But since I am my authentic self, flaws and all, I had to grow into a person who stopped giving a damn about what others did or said to me. Now, this was a process for me because the past trauma in my life caused me to be a major people-pleaser. So much so that I would visualize the approval of others at home, on the job, and even in school. So, as I embarked on what was in my heart to do, imagine how I felt when close friends, coworkers, and family members began to judge me. It was a painful road to travel. But the more I began to embrace and love who I was and who I am becoming, the more I learned that their opinions are theirs. They were entitled to them, but I wouldn't let it stop me from doing what I was passionate about. As I write this book, many of my naysayers who keep my name in their mouths haven't even accomplished half of what I have in this life-time. So, excuse me for a minute if I get raw in my authentic self when I say this; the rapper GloRilla said it best about the naysayers:

"They say they don't fuck with me, but I say THEY CAN'T fuck with me." Enough said.

But just like the little satans, the lowercase "g's" are also assigned to your life. The little gods. People who love you, are rooting for you, and are in your corner. In my trials, I had those types of friends that surrounded me. My family, in the beginning, thought I had lost my mind, but eventu-ally, they came around. Kinda like Job, but you'll see that. Lowercase "g's" however, don't earn that title because they support you. These are people God assigns explicitly to you for a purpose to speak on your behalf when the little devils of this world try to shut you down. One of those people for me is my creative content director. And for this book, I shall call her Sasha.

Sasha and I connected through a mutual friend on a creative assignment. Sasha pulled out of the endeavor, but she and I stayed connected. A few years later, I again reconnected with Sasha during an entrepreneurial endeavor, and she and I became friends. When Sasha met me, I was heavy in the church and in leadership, and I was stepping away. I was in a very emotionally challenging marriage and was about seventy-five pounds overweight. That was the version of me she and others connected with. Fast forward five years, and I'm in the middle of the beginning of my Job experience, which I will discuss in the next chapter. She sees me trying to "manage" the hell I was experiencing. Since Sasha and I had mutual friends in the same circle, you can imagine that the little Satans were in her ear. As a matter of fact, her boyfriend was a mutual connection, someone who knew me as the pouty but talented church girl. She received a lot of backlash for working with me, and although he is a content creator, he refused and had no interest in working with me. He and others I contacted for assistance apparently had an image to uphold. I guess I couldn't blame them. I was entering a world they were unfamiliar with and perhaps didn't morally align. Either way, knowing that someone feels like you don't meet their approval for what you're doing can be hurtful. But in the end, you have to ask yourself, who are they anyway?

When our mutual connections and everyone else out of boredom set a challenge before Sasha, God compelled her to come in and help. God allowed her to see me, see the vision I was trying to create, but could also see where I was going. That is a lowercase g. This is the type of person that I mean. She went against everything the people closest to her were saying to bet on me. And as I write this book, it has definitely begun to pay off. I wonder if their conversation went something like this:

> Naysayers: Girl, I see your girl on social media (shakes head)
>
> Sasha: Yes, I've seen her too
>
> Naysayers: Shameful what she's doing out there. No goal or purpose, just nakedness
>
> Sasha: Well, you know she wrote a book, right? It was really good
>
> Naysayers: Porn...

Sasha: Did you read it?

Naysayers: For what? All that girl is doing is writing nasty stuff and showing all her assets on her OnlyFans page. When she was in church, she had so much promise. What happened?

Sasha: Have you considered that God is not done yet? I feel like God is really gonna use her.

Naysayers: Yea right. She's letting the devil use her right now.

Sasha: Well, let's see what God can do...

And so, it is with the god-assigned folks to you. They speak with the authority and voice of God when Satan dispatches his minions to put their name in your mouth. God will never leave you without help. Have you considered by now who you are to God? Someone special. If God is saying, "Have you considered my servant___," that means that He not only believes but *knows* that whatever in life is thrown at you, that you are genuinely up to the task.

3

WHEN ALL HELL BREAKS LOOSE

What does the term "all hell broke loose" mean? It could mean many different things to different people. All hell breaking loose could be losing multiple loved ones at the same time while you've just broken up with your boyfriend. All hell breaking loose could be finding out that your best friend and your significant other were cheating, and they have a love child. Whatever the hell is, though, it must be something that would make you want to lose your mind. When all hell breaks loose, it's usually more than one thing happening at once, and things spiral quickly out of your control. That's what it means when all hell breaks loose. And when you see what Job went through, you'll understand what I mean.

Before we dive into what Job went through, let's talk about what "all hell breaking loose" is *not*. Little Johnny getting a C in math is not all hell breaking loose. Not being able to get dinner on the table three days in a row and you and your hubby having an argument is not that. Small things happening at once may seem like a lot but put your big girl panties on because you'll know the difference when you see what Job went through and what I describe. When all hell breaks loose, it feels like a series of explosions out of your control. And who is behind it all? God and Satan, according to Chapter 1, Verse 12:

> 12 And the Lord said unto Satan, "Behold, all that
> he hath is in thy power; only upon himself
> put not forth thine hand." So Satan went
> forth from the presence of the Lord.

I know you feel like that's between them, but it has everything to do with you. They say God lives within us; well, sometimes Satan dwells there too. Remember I mentioned when the sons of God approached, and Satan was addressed and not Lucifer? That doesn't mean that Lucifer no longer existed. It simply means that Satan was addressed. Each of us battles with "good and evil," so we must address the God and Satan in each of us. I don't want to get too deep, but we must do this to break down and rebuild our lives into what they're supposed to be. I hate to tell you this, but when all hell breaks loose, there is nothing to do but strap your seatbelt and take the ride.

Now, when all hell breaks loose in your life with God's permission, it's never immediate, although it seems that way. Whenever I was taught in church, I always assumed that right after the discussion, Satan came down and put on a four-corner press on Job. That was not the case. In Verse 13, Satan left the presence of God, but notice Verse 13:

> 13 And there was a day when his sons and his

*daughters were eating and drinking wine in
their eldest brother's house:*

There are two significant things here. First, the word says, "and there was a day," which means some time has passed. How much time we really don't know. Only God and Satan know the answer to that. I have heard scholars indicate that the whole Job trial only lasted thirty days. I find that very interesting and very unbelievable. Yes, I said it. I am not a scholar, but you'll see it took Job over thirty days to go through what he did from beginning to end. Saying Job's trial was that quick and believing it would be like one believing every December 25th that Santa Claus actually travels the globe, squeezes down every chimney, and opens the doors of those who do not (because he doesn't forget about the good children without chimneys, does he?) all in a twenty-four-hour time frame. It's physically impossible for an overweight man with nine flying reindeer to travel the globe. Even when the story originated, it would have been impossible, and again, I say the same about Job's trial. Time had to pass for Satan to enter one realm into another. Time also had to pass because Satan had to have time to study his subject. Satan knew Job like he knows everyone, but when you study your opponent, you look at everything near and dear to them. In war, the best warriors strike at an unexpected time. Don't think Satan came back immediately and attacked Job. He waited until the time was right.

Secondly, here we have his children again, doing what they have been accustomed to doing. They all gathered together doing God knows what at their brother's house. I'm curious and will not speculate, but I believe Job was probably offering burnt offerings if they were all gathered together.

It also tells me things with Job were business as usual, and he had no reason to believe that his world would be rocked. But here comes the storm. If you can relate to Job, take a look at what happened next in verses 14-19 of Chapter 1:

> *14 And there came a messenger unto Job, and said, "The oxen were plowing, and the asses feeding beside them;*
>
> *15 And the Sabeans fell upon them, and took them away; yea, they have slain the servants with the edge of the sword; and I only am escaped alone to tell thee.*
>
> *16 While he was yet speaking, there came also another, and said, 'The fire of God is fallen from heaven, and hath burned up the sheep, and the servants, and consumed them; and I only am escaped alone to tell thee.'*
>
> *17 While he was yet speaking, there came also another, and said, 'The Chaldeans made out three bands, and fell upon the camels, and have carried them away, yea, and slain the servants with the edge of the sword; and I only am escaped alone to tell thee.'*
>
> *18 While he was yet speaking, there came also another, and said, 'Thy sons and thy daughters were eating and drinking wine in their eldest brother's house;*
>
> *19 And, behold, there came a great wind from the wilderness, and smote the four corners of the house, and it fell upon the young men, and they are dead; and I only am escaped alone to tell thee."*

Do you still feel like Job? In a matter of minutes, his lands were attacked and taken over, his animals were stolen, and his children were killed. His livelihood and his family were taken away in an instant. Again, I ask, do you still feel like Job? I don't have to break down these verses because they are self-explanatory. So, when I say Job experience, again, these are big things that feel out of your control. And ARE out of your control. So, the next time some of you compare your trials to Job, here is what he went through—the beginning of his trials.

I want you to be encouraged, though, because God has been gracious enough to some of us to not allow so much at once. Does He not put more on us than we can bear? Looking at Job's experience is designed to take a closer look at the things in your life that have been set before you. So, whatever you have been through, YOUR Job experience, again, I say God knows you are up for the task.

Before I talk about what to do when all hell breaks loose or what Job did anyway, I'll tell you about the beginning of my trials. I had just been promoted to my dream job, making six figures, and had finally separated from my husband. I was experiencing what freedom looked like, and I was traveling a lot with my high-powered job. About ten months into my new position, my husband got into a life-threatening accident and had a new lease on life and wanted me to come back. I reconsidered but kept my separate housing. After a few months, I began to feel uncomfortable again, like something was off. I started having problems balancing my work and family life, and my work began to suffer. I moved back to my apartment and tried to focus on my job. Sixty days later, all hell broke loose in my life. When I moved back into my apartment, I was put on performance review, which had never happened in fifteen years of working with the company. During that time, it was apparent that they wanted to get rid of me. My director removed me from the travel schedule and gave the junior account manager some of my duties. She demanded that I be in the office every day. The only thing she did daily was scrutinize my emails to our client. Imagine me, a writer who had already written a stage play that was accepted at the Atlanta Black Theater Festival, getting her writing skills scrutinized. On one occasion, I resolved a billing issue that had been ongoing for years before I entered the position while on probation, and she appeared unfazed. Outside of scrutinizing my emails, they had nothing else besides the fact that the account executive didn't want me in the position. So, it was no surprise that I was fired within forty-five days of my performance probation. I looked at myself in the mirror, trying to figure out what was next. I had given them fifteen years of my life, only for it to be erased. I called my sister after I saw she had left a text.

My sister Tracie had gone to the hospital to get some tests run. She had been having some bowel problems and said she really wanted someone to visit her. I saw my sister and discovered she would be there for a few days while they ran tests. I had a pleasant visit with my sister and went along my way. A few days later, I had a visit from my former grandchildren. My husband brought them over to announce they would never see me again. I had raised these little ones from birth to ten. I didn't believe what I was hearing until a letter came in the mail. It was a summons for divorce, in which I had to show up in court in a few days. I was shocked because this same man who was begging me to come back to him even the night before had already filed for divorce; go figure.

I started preparing for my divorce. I talked to Tracie, who had just left the hospital. Although saddened, she understood my need for freedom, and I decided when I went to court, I would leave it all behind and start anew. My sister told me she still wasn't feeling well and was going back to the emergency room. She had serious pain in her abdomen and revealed that she had been unable to move her bowels for the past few months; the laxatives and prescriptions she had been given were not working. That trip to the emergency room led to a diagnosis of stage-four colon cancer a week later. Tracie was given about eighteen months to two years to live. I remember my nephew being on the speaker-phone when we got the news. My niece stormed out of the room. I got sick and threw up in the bathroom. Her husband was in shock. My other sister, Tanya, who was in her late forties and dating someone sixteen years her junior, took that time to announce that she was pregnant.

I got home, took a drink, and tried not to think about it. But when nighttime hit, and I was alone with my thoughts, I had the biggest breakdown. As I cried and shook, trying to understand why, I realized so much was happening that I had forgotten I had to be in divorce court the very next day. When I walked out of divorce court, I went to see my sister to get a feel of how she could beat her diagnosis. Tracie was my first best friend, who was only nineteen months older than me. We went through the horrendous trials of life together, and if it weren't for her, I don't know how I would have made it through the early trauma I called my child-hood. I had just lost my job and my marriage; the possibility of losing her was overwhelming.

As I walked into the lobby to my sister's room, I was stopped by her best friend. The night before, we had been putting together Tracie's bucket list of "to-do" things because of her prognosis. Her father and stepmother, Pat, had just gotten into town and were spending time with her. Apparently, while Tracie was away getting more tests run and I was at divorce court, the doctor took that time to address the rest of the family. Tracie's bucket list would have to be shortened significantly. The prognosis was no bucket list at all. There was a massive blockage in her colon, and the cancer had spread to other parts of her body. Her current life expectancy went from eighteen months to ten days. My sister was unaware; her best friend wanted to tell me before I entered the room with the rest of the family. I was heart-broken. Eighteen days later, my sister passed away. The time that passed from me getting fired, the divorce, and my sister passing was only forty-five days. Many of you would have lost your minds. There were times I felt like I wanted to. And just like Job, for me, this was just the beginning.

So, what was Job's response to all of this? Chapter 1, verses 20 and 21:

> 20 Then Job arose, rent his mantle, shaved his
>   head, fell down upon the ground, and
>   worshipped,
> 21 And said, "Naked came I out of my mother's
>   womb, and naked shall I return thither: the
>   Lord gave, and the Lord hath taken away;
>   blessed be the name of the Lord."

The first thing Job did was make some spiritual adjustments. He didn't say, "Why, God?" He didn't go over to his friends' houses and complain; he didn't even drown himself in intoxicating substances. Instead, he fell to the ground and worshipped. Job used the power of affirmations about God. It says, "he said." Do you think he just laid in one spot all day and said, "Glory to God"? No! He affirmed what he knew about God. To do that, he had to take clear actions. He took steps to ensure he was still spiritually aligned with the Creator despite what was happening. You must do the same, no matter what that looks like for you. When all hell starts breaking loose, don't look at the problem or the people, but look to the God within. If you look to God, how you respond will be God-like. Does God operate in fear, shame, or unworthiness? Absolutely not. And how you hold up in your trial will depend on how you arm yourself spiritually. How much do you know about God to sustain you through these significant happenings? When all hell breaks loose, you better know. One thing we do know about Job is this from Chapter 1, Verse 22:

> 22 In all this Job sinned not, nor charged God
>   foolishly.

Whatever was happening, Job knew enough not to blame God for his problems. It's easy for us to do; it can be a cop-out. Yes, it's contradictory because God allows the trial, but we are too quick to blame God for our problems. We're lazy, period. We look to God through prayer to change things and then don't put in the work or actions to turn things around. Then, we have the audacity to get mad at God when things don't change. God is not a magician nor a fairy godfather waving a wand. God is a spirit, so we must connect to God the spirit. We are human and must take action for the things that the spirit reveals. If your life is not what you imagined, don't blame God; He gave you a powerful tool to make things happen for you—your mind. Having had previous success, Job knew that if he tuned into God and did not give into the thoughts that plagued him, this too would pass over, no matter how awful it seemed. So, he worshipped, meditated, and affirmed because, in times like that, what else can you do? Job and I also had something else in common; little did we know this was just the beginning.

4

SOMETIMES YOU HAVE TO LOSE IT
ALL AND LET THE REST GO

As I left off in the last chapter, I mentioned that this was just the beginning for Job. I know you're thinking, "What else could this guy possibly go through?" It seems like he has already lost it all with everything, but the kitchen sink thrown at him. Sometimes, when life gets tough, it feels like the whole house is thrown at you, and for Job, that's precisely what happened next. But first, I need to set up how it happened. Chapter 2 begins:

> *1 Again there was a day when the sons of God*
> *came to present themselves before the Lord,*
> *and Satan came also among them.*
> *2 And the Lord said unto Satan, "From whence*
> *comest thou?" And Satan answered the Lord,*
> *and said, "From going to and fro in the earth,*
> *and from walking up and down in it."*
> *3 And the Lord said unto Satan, "Hast thou*
> *considered my servant Job, that there is none*
> *like him in the earth, a perfect and an upright*
> *man, one that feareth God, and escheweth*

evil? and still he holdeth fast his integrity,
although thou movedst me against him, to
destroy him without cause."

Chapter 2 starts with "Again there was a day," indicating another occasion, right? Absolutely. This implies that some time had passed between all hell breaking loose and losing it all. Satan had to take another occasion to approach the throne again. For the super religious out there, we can agree that if heaven is a real place and God sits on a high throne, then that place cannot be approached at any given time. The "Throne of God" is not like Walmart; you can't come and go as you please. Even the kings and queens of this world serve as a prototype for that.

Additionally, God mentions again how perfect Job is and how he maintained his integrity even though all hell had broken loose. Time had passed. We will never know how much time, but it had to be enough time for God to observe Job's behavior and judge him to be upright. I don't think a week or two is enough time for any human being to prove themselves, but if the scholars still hold fast to the 30-day time frame, so be it.

I also want to pose the question as to what Job was doing between when all hell broke loose and when he felt like he had lost it all. The Bible never really says. At the end of Chapter 1, we know he was in worship, praise, and affirmations. The ending of Chapter 1 indicates that he didn't sin against his creator in all this. So, everything else he was doing had to be assumed. If you were Job, what would you be doing? Would you just lie there in ashes, crying about the situation? Would you call on your closest friends? Remember, he has a handful of servants from his previous properties, only the land he lives on, and his wife. Both have just lost all ten children. What would I be doing if I were Job? I'll tell you.

Unfortunately, when bad things like this happen, if we have breath in our bodies, we still must function. And that's what we do; continue to function. We put ourselves in survival mode. I believe Job did the same thing. Job was the greatest man in the East. So, in addition to not blaming God, he had to grieve and make burial arrangements for his children. I can imagine he also had to be there to comfort his wife. His sons probably left wives and possibly children behind. They needed to be comforted as well. In addition to that, Job had to work on rebuilding his life, trying to get back what he lost. We can only speculate, but if I were Job, I can imagine those were the things he was doing.

Before we get into what happens next with Job, I'll tell you what I did during that time. Like Job, I was trying to find my spiritual grounding. I used daily prayer and visualization. I would take walks near the water and talk to God about my life. Sometimes, I would cry, take nature walks, and hug trees. I was centering myself and finding peace. I also had the task of preparing to bury my sister. One of her last wishes was for me to speak at her homegoing. The other was for me to write a book about our early childhood. I spoke in front of hundreds who loved and adored her and planned to fulfill the other promise for her. I also was trying my best to comfort my loved ones. She left behind my niece, nephew, grandchildren, and siblings who loved her. Her husband moved on in less than six months with my former best friend from my more carefree years. She had the reputation of not only being the town's well-known promiscuous woman, but she was a woman of ill repute in multiple area codes. It was no surprise to most of us that he moved on so quickly, as it was an unspoken fact that he had cheated before. But can you imagine the slap in the face and public humiliation her children faced? Especially in this age of social media.

In addition to all that, I was also trying to rebuild my life or figure it out, anyway. All I knew was I wanted to write and get my creative endeavors back into the world. I had written plays and poetry previously and wanted to challenge myself by writing a book. I also wanted to stretch myself by selecting a genre I had never previously tapped into, erotica. So, I set off on the writing journey, not knowing where this would take me. I just knew that writing was something I was always passionate about doing. While rebuilding my life, I fell in love swiftly with someone sixteen years younger than me. The journey was crazy, beautiful, and amazing. It was also full of laughter, love, heartache, and pain. That man was sent to me for many reasons, and I'm grateful he was there to fuel inspiration and teach tough lessons. But this book is not about that. Just like Job, time had passed before I truly lost it all.

Now, let's go back to the conversation God and Satan were having about Job. When we left off, God was extolling Job's integrity. Well, Satan had a crafty retort:

> 4 And Satan answered the Lord, and said, "Skin
>   for skin, yea, all that a man hath will he give
>   for his life.
> 5 But put forth thine hand now, and touch his
>   bone and his flesh, and he will curse thee to
>   thy face."

> *6 And the Lord said unto Satan, "Behold, he is in*
>   *thine hand; but save his life."*
> *7 So went Satan forth from the presence of the*
>   *Lord, and smote Job with sore boils from the*
>   *sole of his foot unto his crown.*

Satan knew that there was nothing more he could take from Job possession-wise that would make him fold. This infuriated him. So, he thought, surely if I damage this man's body, he will give up and give in. Satan wanted him dead, I'm sure, but how would Job prove himself upright if he were dead? Instead, he did probably the worst thing that can be done to a person who is already struggling mentally, emotionally, and financially—sickness. But isn't that sometimes how it happens? Sometimes, our physical ailments are a result of what we think about. If we focus on sickness, that's what we get, but again, this book is not about that.

So, Job ended up with boils all over his body. Have you ever had one or two boils at the same time? I know I've had one before. Those things are painful. You don't have to touch it for it to hurt; movement or even the wind on a boil can be painful. Boils start as lumps, then fill with pus and eventually drain. Usually, the pus stage occurs after about twenty-four hours. Can you imagine having boils all over your body? First, let's consider his appearance. That is obviously not the most attractive state to be in. Imagine the folks who knew Job the best.

I wonder what they thought when they saw him. Were they horrified? It's hard to see someone perfectly healthy one day and deteriorate the next. Some of us have been there when we have had the task of watching a loved one pass quickly.

My sister Tracie got her diagnosis and passed within eighteen days. Even then, there were not times that I was horrified. But if I were to see her perfectly healthy one day and then the very next day, she looked like she did when she passed, I may have reacted differently. Did his loved ones have a genuine concern for him? I would imagine they did. Some may have even felt sorry for him. What about the rest of the folks in the town? Surely, they had already heard about what had happened to Job previously, and now this? Oh yeah, I know they were talking. Probably secretly judging. Wondering why, if he was such a great man, all this could be happening to him. So, although this part of Job's affliction was physical, there was a lot of psychological and emotional impact behind what he was experiencing. And what about Job's wife? We'll dive into who she was in the next chapter.

So, what did Job do when this happened? Chapter 2, verse 8 says:

> 8 And he took him a potsherd to scrape himself
> withal; and he sat down among the ashes.

The end of verse 10 also says:

> 10 In all this did not Job sin with his lips.

We'll dive more into verse 10 in the next chapter, but Job did two things; he went towards the path to heal himself, and he still allowed no words to come out of his mouth that would blame God for what he was going through. Notice the verse says he did not sin with his lips. Can you imagine his thoughts, though? You know what I'm talking about. Sometimes, thoughts that creep in and speak to us about our situation are not always positive. Your knee starts hurting; your mind wanders about the pain, thinking of all the possibilities of what could be wrong, and the next thing you know, you come to the conclusion that you need a knee replacement. Yes, our thoughts can take us to places we haven't even been or may never even go. So, I'm sure his mind was speaking to him about his current situation and what he had just been through.

The fact that he still didn't allow negativity to come out of his mouth is significant and something you should pay attention to. Job didn't speak negatively because although his mind fed him negative thoughts, he had to choose what to focus on most. He had to gain control of his thoughts. To do that, he had to shut down every negative thought that came to him when it came. We must do the same. When those things enter your mind, shut it down. It takes practice, but as soon as you realize you're thinking negatively, you must arrest that thought. One bad thought will eventually lead to another until it becomes a short film of bad thoughts. Then you wonder why you begin to speak those things and see them play out in your life. Job had to consciously think about his thoughts, which takes intentional practice. But why wait until all hell breaks loose to do that? Job made a practice of this long before the shit began to hit the fan. He was a great man because he knew how to manage his thoughts.

Look at your life and your surroundings. Are you in the middle of a trial? Are you living well or struggling to get where you want to be? The reality is that you have created what you are currently living in some way. So, if you don't like what you see, you must change your thoughts. I'm not exempt from this statement, and to be honest, there have been many times in my own life when I took a hard look around at my life and didn't like what I saw; sometimes, I even hated it. Then, even after KNOWING my life is the sum total of my thoughts, I used to have the audacity to be ANGRY at myself about it. So, I'm preaching to myself as well. When life throws things at you, how you think and respond could be the very difference between life and death for you. However, the light in the tunnel is that as long as you live, you can change your circumstances, no matter how horrible they seem.

So now that we know what happened next with Job, let me take you on an interesting journey of my own. After all those events in the process of rebuilding, ten months later, my world was again turned upside down. I made the decision to part ways with my young lover, and the breakup became toxic. He was the breadwinner; when our love was new, he allowed me to be creative—write, pray, and center myself. In essence, I relied on him to take care of me while I took care of his emotions. He had mommy issues, and eventually, those types of codependent relationships must always come to an end. When I realized it wasn't working, he left me with an apartment I could no longer afford and no way to make an income. I began to Doordash to pay my bills, and it was a struggle. I had completed and self-published my first novel; I was evicted a day before my first book release. At the time, a friend immediately took me in. She was more like family, and I was the godmother to her children. A week later, she put me out of her home. There was no argument or disagreement, and she did it the dirtiest way. After that, she and I didn't speak for a year.

Over the next seven months, I bounced from three different homes, one of which was my ex-lover's, where I stayed the longest. Yes, I was homeless and living with my ex-lover, who I was still getting over the pain and heartache of our separation. What made it more painful was the fact that he was living with another woman. So, I had to endure the uneasiness of watching this man move on and do God knows what with whomever he wanted because I had nowhere else to go. I know it sounds crazy, but God was setting me up for a blessing even in that situation. There were toxic, violent moments between the three of us. It felt like an understatement to say everything about my life was being tested. We had broken up, but it felt like we were still together. I had the only vehicle, so they both used mine. When he needed a vehicle, I gave my contract assignment money to help with his down payment, AND I put his truck in my name. This man had a luxury SUV in my name. Meanwhile, he ran down my vehicle, driving around the city doing illegal activities.

My vision board, affirmations, and belief that I could get out of a situation where I felt trapped kept me grounded in that little room I called my own. When I finally left, even breaking away was violent and toxic. But once COVID hit, a switch went off in my mind, and I was determined NOT to be on lockdown in my current situation. The fighting between him and I, between his lover and him, between the other women I watched him disrespect his lover with, and just all the bad energy as a whole—I knew that being on a complete lockdown during COVID was not going to happen. I thought they could destroy each other, but I knew my life was so much bigger. I don't know how I made it happen, but an apartment opened up for me miraculously, kind of like when the Red Sea parted. I was extremely thankful to be escaping that situation.

Despite what was happening, I continued to ground myself spiritually during those seven months. Every day, I still started my day with prayer and meditation. I expressed gratitude for where I was and the provision that was given. When I lived with my ex, the only belongings in that room that belonged to me were my bed, clothes, laptop, and vision board. I refused to be stuck where I was, and I also refused to blame God for why things were happening the way they were. I knew deep down that in this experience, something extraordinary had to be birthed.

Things started to look up for me. I was in my own space, moving forward, rebuilding. I was able to get back to my writing in a big way. I had written my second novel and even started a podcast. I felt the joy of doing what I loved the most—writing and creating. I gained an audience on social media and was in my element. During COVID, my finances seemed to be recovering. I was moving full steam ahead after hosting a major event in the city and releasing my new book. The two years that had passed didn't feel as painful financially as I was healing from the emotional trauma of the years before. In 2022, things began to get rocky again, but I had written a clear vision for the year ahead.

However, the life I visualized in 2023 was not what happened in 2023. Not by a long shot. At the end of 2022, I had a clear direction for my life. Things were not where I wanted them to be, but I could see a clear path, rebuilding. I was not expecting 2023 to come in like a flood and totally rock my world again. Before 2022 ended, my best friend of almost 25 years, Emma Brown, passed away. I met Emma when I was attending church. Emma was the sweetest and craziest person I had ever met thus far. Emma made me laugh, and I also brought joy to her life. When I met Emma, we were a trio: Emma, myself, and Lisa. Lisa went to another church, and I met her through Emma. We were all single parents and came together many days and nights to pray and fellowship. Emma, Lisa, and their children became my family, and we all did things together. Eventually, both ladies moved away from me, but we kept in touch. Emma and I were still best friends, and when she became sick, I was devastated. Losing my best friend after losing my mother and sister became a lot to bear. The three closest people in my life were no longer there. I felt lonely, and my mind felt like I needed something different to be away from it all.

In February 2023, I had the unction to take a lucrative contract assignment that required travel. I gave up my apartment, and my dog Bentley and I went to see the world. After a month, the work dried up. Imagine being in a hotel room in Saraland, Alabama, in an unfamiliar land with people you don't know. As someone who can pick up on the energy, I saw nothing but despair. I tried to make the situation work, and I even rented a house and tried to find more contract work. The house ended up being roach-infested, and I had to spend money on an exterminator on an already tight budget. I found a temporary remote contract gig and was happy. But, the thought of spending the rest of my life in Alabama was depressing. My options were limited because my rental history had soft evictions from the apartment I just left. Not only that, but I also left my brother in my apartment. In addition to the three soft evictions, I now had a hard eviction on my record. Who in the world would want to rent to me? I figured since I had already stepped out and left Ohio, I might as well land where I wanted, which was Georgia. When I found a room for rent in a suburb of

Atlanta, I thought it was perfect. Atlanta was where I had prayed to land anyway. I met a holistic doctor looking to rent a space to a mature person, and he was also pet-friendly, so Bentley was welcomed. I packed everything that could fit in my Mercedes and headed to Georgia.

When I pulled up to the suburb in Sharpsburg, I was in awe of the beauty. The cheapest home in the neighborhood was worth no less than a half-million, and each home was uniquely landscaped and custom-built. Some had in-ground pools and Jacuzzis. Some had boats and basketball courts. On my walks with Bentley, I even saw a teenage girl running on a custom-built track on their property. In Atlanta, everything was beautiful—the scenery, the sun, the neighborhood. And me, my Mercedes, and Bentley looked right at home there.

Unfortunately, that utopia was very short-lived. My land-lord, a "holistic doctor," seemed helpful initially. He consulted with his African elders about my health and offered holistic solutions. Then, I noticed odd things about his behavior. For one, he never left his bedroom during the day. I wondered if this man was a doctor, what patients would he see? His behavior with me also became a little too friendly with me and other potential tenants. With me, the good doctor would call me into his bedroom early in the morning to ask me questions. His bedroom was on the other side of the house, and when I entered his room, he was lying in bed, apparently naked, under his blanket. I also noticed he had cameras in his bedroom that surveyed most of the house, inside and out. I found that very weird. On one occa-sion, he asked me to meet him in the living room, a mutual area, to have a conversation about our leasing agreement. When I arrived in the living room, he was sitting on the chair with nothing but a bath towel. He stood up, turned his back towards me, and adjusted his towel. I was in shock. This man would also try texting me during my work hours, demanding that I converse with him. My biggest relief was the fact that he was interviewing other tenants. Whenever there was a tenant interview, it was always a female. Somehow, that female ended up being there all day. And in the case of the newest soon-to-be tenant, she spent several nights in that man's bedroom before he decided she could move in. That must have been one heck of an interview.

This man also seemed very jealous and controlling—jealous that I was a published author while he struggled to keep the discipline to get his thoughts on paper. He tried to belittle my accomplishments by saying I was still "aspiring" and knew nothing about the literary world. He loved to throw in my face that he was a doctor and was visibly upset when he found out I had another book coming out. He even told me I shouldn't have released another book until the first one was successful. The egg was on his face when my new book was released. It was number two hundred on Amazon's bestseller list, and I was expecting future-dated royalties in the thousands. I never told him how well the release of my book was going; I just let him think what he wanted. After all, outside of a room in a beautiful house that was starting to feel like a prison, this man held no value to my life whatsoever.

However, the final straw for me was when the good doctor entered my personal bathroom without my permission. I was going out that night, and he knew that. It was my girlfriend's birthday weekend, and after a few errands, I headed to the shower to get ready. My shower had one of those see-through doors and no shower curtain. As I was showering, he opened my bathroom door and came in to ask a question. Imagine the horror I felt as my naked body was exposed to this man. He acted like it was no big deal, which was a problem for me. I decided then and there that this arrangement was not working. I prayed for an out, as I had literally just signed the lease.

My out came as a contract assignment that required me to be physically located back in my hometown. I called my daughter, packed what I could in my Mercedes, and left the rest behind; once again, I was leaving things behind. The eight-hour drive ended up being eleven hours, and then I stayed up the next twenty-four hours just processing the trauma I had been through. I took my belongings up into the spare room of my daughter's apartment and set up what would become my life for now. I had a laptop, an air mattress, and a few clothing items—that was it. I had about fifty dollars to my name but was hopeful. After my body finally crashed from the travel and the trauma, I finally got some rest. The following day, I took Bentley for a walk. Our walks together were the one thing that was our solace throughout this whole ordeal. Walking is how we bonded, and at that moment, I not only thought about my own trauma but perhaps my dog had been through his own trials because of what was happening to me. My whole life seemed so overwhelming at that time because I had lost everything.

As Bentley and I approached the apartment, I felt refreshed. A good walk does that for you. In the distance, I saw a tow truck approaching, which I paid no mind—until it pulled right up to the back of my Mercedes. They were coming to get Meagan. I couldn't blame them; I was behind on the payments at this point. I loved my Mercedes. Meagan was the first car on my vision board. I should have been devastated, but after everything I had been through, I simply didn't care anymore. At first, I wanted to pool all my money together to save myself. But I thought, what would I be saving? Humiliation from others? My own pride? As they pulled away with Meagan, I laughed out loud. I had truly lost it all and perhaps my mind by now. I shrugged my shoulders, took Bentley into the house, and took a deep breath in and out. I thanked God for a roof over my head, food on the table, and people who loved me. When you lose it all, you have to let the rest go.

Letting the rest go. What does that mean? It means just surrender. When you've done all that is in your power, surrender. When you can't do anything else, surrender. Let it all go. Everything. And just like Job, what did I do? The only thing I knew how to do was center myself spiritually. What else was left? When I lost my car, I was left with two options that I gladly took: borrowing my daughter's car, which I had given her on occasion, and walking. Since my daughter had her own obligations, I tried to keep option one at a minimum. Walking to my destination, I began to mull over what was happening with gratitude. And in those moments, God began to speak to me about Job. I told you I didn't choose the assignment to write this book; it was impressed upon my heart over and over again. In some ways, I felt like I lost it all, and then some, like Job. But I was not expecting to share my thoughts and what I got from them with the world. But who else is there to listen to when you lose it all?

5

YOUR INNER CIRCLE: WHO'S THERE?

When we go through these big trials, although it feels like we are walking alone, we are truly not. If bad things are happening to you, the things that are happening are also impacting the ones closest to you as well. It is selfish and unrealistic to think you are utterly alone in what is happening to you. If a loved one dies, you are not the only one impacted by that loss. If you lose your job—even if you are single—someone else is impacted: your former employer, clients, etc. So, what I'm basically saying is this: don't fall into the trap of thinking you are all by yourself. Even the things I shared about my trials are not unique to me alone. Someone else can relate to some of what I have been through, if not all.

Job also was not alone, as we will begin to see. He had a few people he communicated with throughout this book in the Bible, and I'll call them his inner circle. Your inner circle are those who are the closest to you. They could be anyone. Some are friends, family members, co-workers, and the like, but these people have your ear and heart. Your inner circle usually consists of a handful of folks. These are the people that you let into your private world. These are the folks who really get to see you for who you are—the ones you feel safe letting your hair down around. Your inner circle should be the people you trust the most in life. Job had such folks also, and for him, this is where it gets interesting.

One key thing to point out here—and pay attention to this: Notice how, in Chapter One, things moved very quickly regarding describing what happened to Job. Chapter Two also begins hot and heavy and right into his second trial. But we will see that the rest of the book of Job slows COMPLETELY down, and the writer takes their time describing the interaction between:

1. Job and his inner circle
2. Job and God

This is very telling. It tells me that you always need to be aware of who your core folks are. What do they believe? How do they talk? Are they people who will push you forward, or are they happy in your misery? They say if you want to know who YOU truly are, look at the five people you surround yourself with most. Pause and take a minute to do that. Who do you talk to the most? What do you talk about? Do you discuss people, or do you discuss ideas? Who you surround yourself with is extremely important. When you go through things, you'll sometimes, unfortunately, see what and who your circle truly is. Job was not exempt from this.

> 7 So went Satan forth from the presence of the
> Lord, and smote Job with sore boils from the
> sole of his foot unto his crown.

> *8 And he took him a potsherd to scrape himself*
> *withal; and he sat down among the ashes.*
> *9 Then said his wife unto him, Dost thou still*
> *retain thine integrity? curse God, and die.*

> — JOB 2:7-9, KJV

The person closest to Job was his wife. What counsel did she provide? She tells him basically to go ahead and die. Not only that, she said to curse God and die. This tells me she had reached her own breaking point. But it also tells me what kind of support she had as well. Who was in her ear? If you want to get spiritual, you can say Satan, of course. She told him to do the very thing that Satan said that Job would do to God. So, of course, Satan had something to do with it. I told you what happens to you impacts others. Don't you think she was impacted? She lost all her kids, her man had lost his financial means, and now he has a disease that has pretty much taken him out, and all he wants to do is isolate himself. I can guarantee that Job went into hermit mode; he had to go completely within. So, what was his wife to do but seek the counsel closest to her? And from her response to his situation, she obviously was not seeking wise counsel. In modern-day times, I would venture to say that Job's wife had "chicken heads" as her inner circle. If you don't believe me, look how Job answered her next in verse ten of the same chapter:

> *10 But he said unto her, Thou speakest as one of*
> *the foolish women speaketh. What? shall we*
> *receive good at the hand of God, and shall we*
> *not receive evil? In all this did not Job sin*
> *with his lips.*

He told her, first off, to watch her mouth. She sounded like the 'foolish women' in the village. Who do you think she was talking to about her problems?

> Friends: GIRL! What's going on over there?

> > Mrs. Job: I don't know y'all. Why is this happening to me?

> Friends: It's your man, girl! Look at him! First, y'all lost the kids, the property, and now he got leprosy, girl! Think about it!

> > Mrs. Job: Now wait a minute...

> Friends: No, YOU wait a minute. All this bad stuff is happening to HIM! You need to be asking God what he did to be CURSED!

And so, Job's wife probably marinated on it because of her counsel until she had her breaking point.

Thank goodness Job didn't listen to his wife. He essentially told her that God allows both the good and the bad in our lives. Are we once again treating infinite intelligence like a genie? Do we really think that life is going to be all good and not bad? That belief system itself destroys the law of balance. There are certain laws in place in this world that cannot and will not be broken. The law of gravity is one of them. Can you expect to jump off an airplane with no parachute and survive? Heck no! So, unfortunately, good cannot exist without the bad. Ask yourself honestly, are you all good all the time? If you answered yes, you're a liar, and the truth isn't in you. Some of you lie, gossip, and cross lines that only you and God know about. The light of God is not in those things. So, how dare we think that because something bad is happening, God is not working in it? Thinking that you are not going to experience grief, pain, and heartache in life is like thinking that the sun is always supposed to shine and that the moon is not needed. Bad things are going to happen, and you may not understand why. The lesson in the bad things happening is taking a deeper dive within. Looking at you. A lot of people want to blame people and circumstances for why they aren't happy with their own lives. But you must ask yourself what actions you took during those bad times.

Well, we know what Job did. In all that, he STILL maintained his integrity by allowing no bad thing to come out of his mouth about the situation. How many of us can honestly say that—let's be honest. Many of us are itching to tell at least one person what's happening just to get it off our chest. I know I have. I called my girlfriend like, "You won't believe what's happening to me!" and passed that energy off to the next person. Shameful. I'm not condemning you; I'm talking to myself here, but Job kept his mouth shut. He had to have a certain level of mental discipline to accomplish this. I'm sure some of the thoughts in his head were contrary to what came out of his mouth. His own mind probably told him to curse God. But Job tapped into a secret that many of us bypass; he arrested his thoughts.

I mean that Job lived a lifestyle of prayer, meditation, and affirmations. Every time bad things happened, he turned to his spiritual practice. Consistent affirmations serve as a tool to reprogram your mind. When you consistently affirm good things, when the negative thoughts filter in, you can identify them quickly and counter them with positive ones. It was easy for Job to say good things about God because he spoke those things daily. Some people only exercise these practices when all hell breaks loose; honestly, that is not enough to sustain you. You will never be who you came to be in this life if you only call on spirituality during hard times. If the creator could be offended, I believe creation would be offended by that. Imagine having a significant other that only came around when things were going well for you. When the rubber hits the road, imagine them leaving you alone and destitute. Then, as you struggle in triumph to pick yourself up, they return with promises of doing better because they need you. You fall again, and they desert you again. And the cycle repeats again and again. That's how we are with the creator sometimes. The good news is that God is patient and kind. He waits for us to get it together.

The closest person in Job's inner circle was his wife. We see she was not supportive of him. As a matter of fact, his wife is not mentioned anymore in this book of the Bible. All she got was one verse. I can only speculate that she left him shortly after that. Think about it; she had unwise women in her ear providing her counsel. This tells me she probably has always had that, which could have been a source of contention in their marriage. I'm just speculating, of course. And if Job's wife did leave him, hear this clearly. When women leave a situation, they have already emotionally checked out. Most women who are reading this will agree. How long she has been emotionally unattached from Job is really the question. Emotional check-outs usually take a build-up of years. So, Job's wife could have emotionally checked out of the marriage long before the trial began. Again, I am only giving you something to think about here, so don't stone me in your mind because I'm just speculating. I do believe, though, that she left him because I can't imagine that Job would have divorced her. He had too much going on, especially since his health was impacted. All Job wanted her to do was get her mind right and stand with him in his darkest time. Job's wife probably moved on to the next best thing in the city with the help of her girlfriends, of course. I'm not saying this happened. I'm just speculating.

Even with the arrival of Job's friends, there is no mention of her.

Now, speaking of Job's friends, I have my own personal insight as to what was happening with them, his inner circle. You may or may not agree, but I'll save that for a bit later. So, at this point, Job has lost his whole family and his livelihood and is now stricken with sickness. His friends think it's time to pay him a visit in Chapter 2, verse 11:

> *11 Now when Job's three friends heard of all this*
> *evil that had come upon him, they came each*
> *one from his own place; Eliphaz the Teman-*
> *ite, and Bildad the Shuhite, and Zophar the*
> *Naamathite: for they had made an appoint-*
> *ment together to come to mourn with him*
> *and to comfort him.*

Let's break this down and bust the whole thirty-day Job trial myth again. First, his friends had to get wind of what was happening to him. Back then, how was communication spread? Primarily by men traveling on horses or camels. They lived in different places, so I'm sure they all got the news at various times. Not only that, the text indicates that they made an appointment to come together at the same time. How much time passed before they got the news, coordinated their efforts, and decided to meet? They were all in different countries and lands, remember. Some may have had to travel by sea, who knows. The point of the story is they all came together as one in the "support" of their good friend, Job.

> 12 And when they lifted up their eyes afar off, and
> knew him not, they lifted up their voice and
> wept; and they rent every one his mantle, and
> sprinkled dust upon their heads toward
> heaven. So they sat down with him upon the
> ground seven days and seven nights, and
> none spake a word unto him: for they saw
> that his grief was very great.

Notice when his friends arrive that his wife is not mentioned. They see Job from afar, and Job's appearance is unrecognizable to them. I'm sure it was heartbreaking for them to see him like this. But they saw him alone. Job's wife was gone. Immediately, they prayed for their friend, as a good religious person should. This makes me wonder if Job had religious tendencies himself from time to time. He atoned religiously for his children up until the day of their death. Observing his closest friends and how they shared their perspectives may give us a deeper insight into how he might have thought at times. How can we grow beyond the strongest people in our circle? Perhaps Job was the strongest in his, which could be dangerous. You never want to be the smartest or most powerful person in the room; there's no room to expand if you are. Perhaps this is what God was trying to teach Job through this trial from the beginning. I believe so, and sometimes expansion is uncomfortable, and that's the biggest myth we choose to hold onto.

I'm sure Job's intercession from his friends was a collaborative effort well before they approached him—you know how church folks are, "Look at our downtrodden brother, we need to pray," and not knowing what they truly should be praying about. I wonder how much time they spent praying on his behalf while or before it happened. Or was this the first time they pooled their efforts for him when they saw the state he was truly in? The Bible then says they didn't speak to him for seven days because they knew he was in so much grief. In my opinion, their silence was probably the best thing they could have done. But we all know that when bad things happen, those closest to us must shed a little light on things of their own. But at least they were respectful enough to let Job express himself first. In Chapter Three, Job begins to speak:

> *1 After this, Job opened his mouth and cursed*
>   *his day.*
> *2 And Job spoke, and said,*
> *3 Let the day perish wherein I was born, and the*
>   *night in which it was said, There is a man-*
>   *child conceived.*

Notice that he blamed himself and not God. Job said many other things in this chapter, but you'll have to read all that yourself. The short version is he was cursing everything about himself, his entry into this world, his mother's pain, and so on. "Curse" is a harsh word, but at that point, Job wished for death, which seemed preferable to what he was enduring. Some of you have been there. I often hear it in the life insurance industry with older clients waiting to go to the promised land. They are tired of life and think death would be better. Some of the things you and I have gone through have taken us to a breaking point where, when some of us open our eyes, we cry because we're still here. I say "we" as a collective, but I know what that pain feels like. When Job finally spoke and said he wished he hadn't been born, I'm sure his friends looked at him as if he felt sorry for himself because it's very easy to look at someone else's situation and tell them to stand strong. In my humble opinion, saying nothing was still the best thing they could have done, and you'll see why. What Job said next was probably the final straw for his friends, in verse twenty-five:

> 25 For the thing which I greatly feared is come
> upon me, and that which I was afraid of is
> come unto me.
> 26 I was not in safety, neither had I rest, nor was
> I quiet; yet trouble came.

Before we move on, we must address the obvious; Job had real fears, too. The verse says, "the thing he feared, and that which he was afraid of." So, Job had an innate fear of losing it all. We know fear begins in our thoughts and in the mind. Although he religiously offered burnt offerings on behalf of his family, there was a fear of losing them. Job probably feared his wife would eventually move on long before she did. Being known as the greatest man in the East probably came with a certain amount of pressure that induced some level of fear. The level of calamity that Job experienced had to be a buildup of his fears over time. The same is true for you and me; we are no different. I know you have rehearsed a bad thing in your mind, and when it happened, you thought to yourself, "I knew it!" Well, you really must ask yourself how often you rehearsed that fear or thought about it over and over in your mind until a version of it happened. If I can use an honest example from my own life, I will; there is no shame in my game.

When I was married, a part of me was miserable for a very long time. I focused on what was wrong in the marriage and how wrong my husband was. I eventually emotionally checked out and sometimes pictured myself getting a divorce. The thoughts started small during little arguments, then spoke louder during hard times. I sometimes saw myself leaving the situation and pictured many different divorce scenarios throughout the years. Eventually, I moved out, and my ex-husband filed for divorce within six months of my leaving. I had the audacity to be slightly surprised, although I had emotionally moved on. Why should I have been surprised when I had rehearsed that in my mind periodically throughout the years? Pay attention to what you are thinking about. What is it that you are currently rehearsing? What is your current situation, or what are the potential outcomes? I'm sure Job's fear of losing it all didn't go down exactly how he imagined it. He probably imagined the same fear in different scenarios. You can change the potential outcome of your life by focusing on the outcomes and not your fears.

I mentioned earlier that Job's outburst did not sit well with his friends. Eliphaz was the first to speak, and it's interesting what he says in Chapter Four:

> *1 Then Eliphaz the Temanite answered and said,*
> *2 If we assay to commune with thee, wilt thou be grieved? But who can withhold himself from speaking?*
> *3 Behold, thou hast instructed many, and thou hast strengthened the weak hands.*
> *4 Thy words have upheld him that was falling, and thou hast strengthened the feeble knees.*

> 5 But now it has come upon thee, and thou
>   faintest; it toucheth thee, and thou art
>   troubled.

Eliphaz could not WAIT to speak his peace. This friend of his had obviously been pondering Job's dilemma and had his own thoughts as to why this was happening to him. He knew Job was a great man and a good friend who had been a source of strength to many, but seeing him like this was probably shocking. And being the religious man that Eliphaz appeared to be, his religious mind could not comprehend that his brother and friend needed to be strengthened. It was almost as if he was making light of Job's situation. He basically said, "You're so good at helping others, but now that you're going through, you're folding. What's up with that?" He's asking him where the same faith he had for others is. I don't know about you, but if I were Job and I had just lost my wife, family, and possessions, I surely wouldn't want my closest friends to tell me to toughen up. That's the last thing I need to hear. Job was probably thinking, 'I'm breathing, dammit, that makes me tough!' Not only did Eliphaz tell him he shouldn't be surprised by what is happening, but he then goes on to imply that bad things don't happen to good people in verses six through nine:

> 6 Is not this thy fear, thy confidence, thy hope,
>   and the uprightness of thy ways?
> 7 Remember, I pray thee, who ever perished,
>   being innocent? Or where were the righteous
>   cut off?
> 8 Even as I have seen, they that plow iniquity,
>   and sow wickedness, reap the same.

> *9 By the blast of God they perish, and by the*
> *breath of his nostrils are they consumed.*

If I were Job, I would have, at this point, been questioning my whole existence. My close friend who came to support me is now telling me that I must be evil, or my actions somehow led to this calamity. At least, that would be what I would think if my closest confidants came to me this way. It feels like judgment, and I wouldn't want folks who are supposed to provide comfort giving judgment instead. Let me take a moment to address something. As a friend, sometimes your truth comes off as judgment. People sometimes think that as friends, that gives them the right to say whatever they want to you, and you should be ok with it because that's how they feel. Keep your feelings to yourself sometimes because you are still on the outside looking in on the situation. The trial is not happening to you just because you can see from the outside. Your friend going through the trial is praying MORE about their own life situation than you are. Be there as a friend to support, not judge.

Eliphaz took it a step further by sharing what "God showed him" about Job's situation in verses thirteen through seventeen:

> *13 In thoughts from the visions of the night, when*
> *deep sleep falleth on men,*
> *14 Fear came upon me, and trembling, which*
> *made all my bones to shake.*
> *15 Then a spirit passed before my face; the hair of*
> *my flesh stood up:*
> *16 It stood still, but I could not discern the form*

> *thereof: an image was before mine eyes, there*
> *was silence, and I heard a voice, saying,*
> 17 *'Shall mortal man be more just than God?*
> *Shall a man be more pure than his maker?*

Isn't it amazing how much God speaks to us about everybody else's situation? I thought God dwelled within us all. Why would God speak to Eliphaz about Job and not to Job? Wasn't this happening to him? Eliphaz represents those super-spiritual folks in our lives who always have a word from God for somebody else. We all know who they are. Eliphaz took it a step further and gave his advice because, of course, he wouldn't be a good friend if he didn't in verses eight and nine:

> 8 *I would seek unto God, and unto God would I*
> *commit my cause:*
> 9 *Which doeth great things and unsearchable;*
> *marvelous things without number.*

"Just pray, Job." That's what he was saying. "Have you sought God to find out why this is happening?" I would seek the Lord. Eliphaz, what do you think he's been doing all this time? Tell Job something that he did not know. That's what Job was looking for. Job was doing all he KNEW to do, and so far, friend number one had no additional insight. Job responds by internalizing what he did to bring this on himself. You can read all that for yourself in Chapter seven. Job's response to Eliphaz was, 'Help me figure out the actions to turn this situation around; don't tell me what I did wrong to deserve this.' He said, 'Don't judge me, give me answers.'

Well, his second friend Bildad didn't really like how Job responded to Eliphaz, so he began expressing himself in Chapter eight:

> *1 Then answered Bildad the Shuhite, and said,*
> *2 How long wilt thou speak these things? And how long shall the words of thy mouth be like a strong wind?*
> *3 Doth God pervert judgment? Or doth the Almighty pervert justice?*
> *4 If thy children have sinned against him, and he have cast them away for their transgression;*
> *5 If thou wouldest seek unto God betimes, and make thy supplication to the Almighty;*
> *6 If thou wert pure and upright; surely now he would awake for thee, and make the habitation of thy righteousness prosperous.*

Now, Bildad's approach was a bit more direct. He wasn't playing with Job. Have you ever met that righteous friend of yours who always KNOWS what they know? Or perhaps he felt that since they were friends, he was liberated to speak his peace, no holds barred—we have friends like that, too. Bildad summed these verses up in a few ways. He was bold and made Job challenge everything about himself. He said, "Job if you were as righteous as you thought you were, this surely wouldn't be happening to you!" Job had lost everything. So, was Bildad indicating Job's family wasn't righteous? In a passive-aggressive way, yes. Was he saying that, somehow, Job contributed to his financial losses and everything else? Oh, absolutely. Bildad's response was that God makes no mistakes, so get right with God and CHECK YOURSELF! That's all Bildad had to offer. Bildad offered more of his opinion than support or advice. I think we've all had those kinds of friends and family members. Opinions are not valid if they don't help to create solutions.

Now, Job responds to him with acknowledgment and agreement but pleads his case in Chapter Nine:

> *1 Then Job answered and said,*
> *2 I know it is so of a truth: but how should man be just with God?*
> *3 If he will contend with Him, he cannot answer Him one of a thousand.*
> *4 He is wise in heart, and mighty in strength: who hath hardened himself against Him, and hath prospered?*

Job says, "I get what you're saying. Get right with God. But HOW? How can I, Bildad? Please tell me." If I were Job, I would have said that with a little more pizzazz. I felt Job's frustration with his friend. Job was doing all he knew to do in the face of a series of tragic events, and all his friend had to offer was, "Get right with God?" On top of that, you have no idea how to do that? Bildad should have told Job, "You know you ain't right; get your life right," like some saints do. No solutions, just a simple "Get it together," which he had been doing through all of this. If it were not so, God would not have judged his uprightness, remember? When Bildad came hard, Job stood his ground and summed it up this way:

1. What do you think I've been doing?
2. Tell me something I don't already know.
3. Let me tell you what I know about God.

4. It feels like God is not speaking. Maybe I cannot hear. If God chooses not to answer, what am I supposed to do?
5. I'm tired.

Does any of this sound familiar to you? That same cycle of emotions that Job felt? Tell me you haven't felt like this before. Doing everything in your power, you know to do. Then your friends provide hollow advice, not knowing how much effort and prayer you have put into finding the answers. When someone says something like, "Just pray, or you know your life ain't right," are they assuming that you haven't been doing the things to get your life in order? Let me put this in a better perspective for you. One example that comes to mind is a woman trying to conceive. She and her partner have no idea what the problem is, but they've been trying for years.

Along with prayer and specialist visits, they still seem unsuccessful. The woman is feeling hopeless as she watches all her friends celebrate pregnancy and childbirth throughout the years through pain-filled eyes. She reaches a place of hopelessness, and her girlfriends, who already have children, come to her side. Imagine if one of those women said, "Girl, what's going on over here? If you don't have a baby yet, it's obviously something you're doing. Pray and get your life together. God obviously doesn't think you're ready yet." I'm sure that kind of response would sting for the woman who only wanted to experience motherhood once in life but hasn't been successful so far. And to have the message delivered by a friend. A better response would have been to simply pray for and WITH them. As a friend, if you can't do anything else, do that.

Job also had to remember what he knew about God. In the roughest of times, your faith will be challenged by the people closest to you, and you must remember what you know about God, whatever that may be. Now, this is not religious. Religion says you must perform acts of all sorts to know about God. God is within. So, you already know about God. Job had to go deep within and remember who God was to him. The question for you should be, who is God to you? What has God represented in your life? When have you been brought through previous tough times, how did the God within offer the solution? Going through hard times challenges you to take a magnifying glass to those areas of your life that make you uncomfortable. Hard times magnify the pain. It's in those times that we must dig deep within.

But what if it feels like God is not speaking? We've been there too, haven't we? Why can't I hear God? Sometimes, we can't hear because we haven't created the space to hear God. Sometimes, the space we have created in the trial is not conducive for the God within to make themselves available. Or perhaps God isn't speaking because the time is not for speaking but for going through the fire to come out refined.

It could be any of those scenarios, and it could be other reasons. Your experience is unique, so if God is not speaking, the answers why are within you. Get quiet just a little bit every single day. If you have been still and silent, take a little more time; be more still. God does not withhold information that we need from us. God is not like that. You are loved, and God loves you, and He knows that whatever you are experiencing, this is not your end but only the beginning.

Lastly, Job indicates that he is tired. This trial had whooped his ass. I know you've been there, doing all you can do in your own power, only for life to keep throwing you curve balls. I have wanted to throw my hands up so many times before. However, being tired is a good place to be, believe it or not. Now, I didn't say being tired FEELS good. I said it's a good place to be. In that valley of despair, you have two options; stay there or take action and continue to believe that things will turn around for you. See, you can't give up. Have you ever heard of the analogy of being "Three feet from gold?" If you haven't, it simply means that you have gotten so close to your dream, escape, or breakthrough, but you don't realize it. Why? Sometimes, you still don't have the answers, and the people around you are not wise enough to provide solutions. We'll see this as his next friend speaks and says much more. Allow me to introduce you to Zophar in Chapter Eleven:

> *1 Then answered Zophar the Naamathite, and said,*
> *2 Should not the multitude of words be answered? And should a man full of talk be justified?*
> *3 Should thy lies make men hold their peace? And when thou mockest, shall no man make thee ashamed?*
> *4 For thou hast said, My doctrine is pure, and I am clean in thine eyes.*
> *5 But oh that God would speak, and open His lips against thee;*
> *6 And that He would show thee the secrets of wisdom, that they are double to that which is! Know therefore that God exacteth of thee less than thine iniquity deserveth.*

So, Zophar's conversation is very interesting. Let's not skim over the fact that Job had expressed himself in this emotional cycle that we all seem to go through, and Zophar doesn't even acknowledge his pain. Zophar shows no compassion for what Job is going through. He basically tells Job in verse one that he is full of himself for justifying his actions to his friends. He thinks Job is delusional and lying to himself about his situation. He also accuses Job of being righteous in his own eyes and wonders what God would say about the matter if Job spoke to Him. Unbeknownst to Zophar, God allowed Job these trials and circumstances because He knew what Job could handle. That's pure audacity if you ask me. You tread dangerous territory when you assume for all of creation. We must be cautious in believing that God is not with them because someone is having a hard time.

Zophar then offered useless advice, just like the two friends before, in verses thirteen through twenty:

> 13 If thou prepare thine heart, and stretch out
>   thine hands toward him;
> 14 If iniquity be in thine hand, put it far away,
>   and let not wickedness dwell in thy
>   tabernacles.
> 15 For then shalt thou lift up thy face without
>   spot; yea, thou shalt be steadfast, and shalt
>   not fear:
> 16 Because thou shalt forget thy misery, and
>   remember it as waters that pass away:
> 17 And thine age shall be clearer than the noon-
>   day: thou shalt shine forth, thou shalt be as
>   the morning.

> *18 And thou shalt be secure, because there is hope;*
> *yea, thou shalt dig about thee, and thou shalt*
> *take thy rest in safety.*
> *19 Also thou shalt lie down, and none shall make*
> *thee afraid; yea, many shall make suit unto*
> *thee.*
> *20 But the eyes of the wicked shall fail, and they*
> *shall not escape, and their hope shall be as the*
> *giving up of the ghost.*

So let me summarize this great advice for you; Zophar said, pray Job, and you'll feel much better. If you don't feel better, the world will know where you stand with God. Only folks who don't know God wish to die, but God's children know that He won't put more on you than you can bear. So now, Zophar comes off as the expert on how God operates. We all know that type, don't we? A lot of these "over-religious" folks who love to speak on "your" trial have never been through what YOU have been through. A person who has never experienced extreme poverty can never understand what it's like to go through that. Yet, in circumstances like that, they feel they need to speak. Again, sometimes the best way to support those going through Job-like trials is not to add your input.

Job responds to his friend in Chapter twelve:

> *1 And Job answered and said,*
> *2 No doubt but ye are the people, and wisdom*
> *shall die with you.*
> *3 But I have understanding as well as you; I am*
> *not inferior to you: yea, who knoweth not*
> *such things as these?*

Job tries to be cordial here, but I believe he has had enough. If I were Job, I would feel like Zophar was insulting my intelligence. Job essentially tells him, "Thank you for your words of so-called wisdom, but good sir, you are no better than me." He tried to make Job feel inferior because of what he was going through. At least Job felt that way. If you don't believe me, he mentions this to Zophar again in Chapter thirteen:

> 1 Lo, mine eye hath seen all this, mine ear hath
>   heard and understood it.
> 2 What ye know, the same do I know also: I am
>   not inferior unto you.

Job got a little edgy here, essentially saying that everything Zophar shares is pretty elementary knowledge. But Job was not done with him or the other two in verses three through five:

> 3 Surely I would speak to the Almighty, and I
>   desire to reason with God.
> 4 But ye are forgers of lies, ye are all physicians of
>   no value.
> 5 O that ye would altogether hold your peace! and
>   it should be your wisdom.

There it is, what I said from the beginning. Job felt like his friends' words of comfort held no value for him. They should have kept their mouths shut. My mother used to say, "If you don't have anything nice to say, don't say it at all." How different would the outcome have been if they had just gathered around him and truly comforted him? As humans, we always think we can fix things. Their conversation broke him down more than it built him up. Your relationships with the people closest to you should not be draining, especially when facing adversities. Take this time to truly look at the five people you interact with most and ask yourself, are they helping you grow, or do they hinder the work you are trying to do in your life?

Now Job had a lot more to say because Zophar insulted his intelligence. Let's look at verses seven through ten:

> 7 *Will ye speak wickedly for God? and talk deceit-*
>   *fully for him?*
> 8 *Will ye accept his person? will ye contend*
>   *for God?*
> 9 *Is it good that he should search you out? or as*
>   *one man mocketh another, do ye so*
>   *mock him?*
> 10 *He will surely reprove you if ye do secretly*
>   *accept persons.*

Job flat-out asks Zophar if he is God because he clearly feels like he can speak on behalf of Him. I wonder if Zophar was one of those people who always have a word from the "Lord" for someone else and not for themselves. You must be cautious with that type. God speaks through whom He wants to, but He will always speak to you more about you and the things that pertain to you. God did not design us to seek answers outside ourselves on a primary level through people. We have access to the Creator because He lives within us all. If God lives within, He desires us to GO within for answers. So, relying on hearing God through others can cause you to become enabled and open the door to deception. In verse thirteen, Job asks them to shut up and leave him alone:

> *13 Hold your peace, let me alone, that I may*
> *speak, and let come on me what will.*

I believe Job was extremely frustrated with his friends at this point. Job was trying to get them to understand what was happening to him in REAL TIME. None of Job's friends had ever walked through a fraction of what he did. Look at how each of them responded. No compassion, no empathy, just opinions and advice for him. Notice I said advice, not solutions. To make matters worse, his friends did not stop; they continued to insist that Job brought all this calamity on himself. If you don't believe me, this conversation between Job and his friends goes on and on until they finally give up nineteen chapters later in Chapter thirty-two:

> *32 So these three men ceased to answer Job,*
> *because he was righteous in his own eyes.*

Why do you think Job's friends stopped talking? I can probably guess they were at a loss for words. Job felt justified, and there was nothing more they could say to him. I can imagine that they were furious. The plan they devised did not work out well for them. My personal opinion on this meeting between Job and his friends was not one of them came together and prayed for their brother's strength. These men were coming together for an intervention. An intervention, by basic definition, is the act of interfering with the outcome or course of something with the intention of improving a condition or process. Job's friends felt like he must have been on a path of destruction, so as his friends, it was their job to get him back on course. Think about it, these three men communicated and coordinated their efforts prior to seeing Job. There is no mention that Job knew his friends were coming. They came together first and prayed, which was their strategy for approaching the situation. Then, when the time was right, they sat with him, and each of them waited to speak their peace. Each friend made sure to get their point across, and the fact that the back and forth went on for over twenty chapters sets up like an intervention. His friends stood their ground. Job did what any person in an intervention-type situation would do; defend themselves when caught off guard. Job was expecting support from his friends. He would have better prepared himself if he knew his friends were coming and could have predicted the outcome.

Before I move on to the next person who spoke, let me share a little about my experience with so-called friends during my trial. As I struggled and DoorDash was my only income, my friends told me I needed to get a job. I also had a so-called social media acquaintance try to ruin my name on social media because of her jealousy over men she had dated many years prior who had shown an interest in me. I was doing many live videos and gaining a following at this time. I was writing my book and trying to piece my life together in the middle of love's heartache. This "so-called" friend belittled the fact that I was delivering food and tried to paint the picture on social media that I was a no-good man-stealing whore. When my so-called friend of almost twenty-five years put me out of her home, she spread nasty rumors about me.

I also had people I used to connect with in the church talk about me among themselves. I've had family members stop talking to me, and close friends of the family suddenly decided that they no longer liked me. Women mostly, which was very shocking to me. I guess it shouldn't have been, considering I was writing erotica and had my half-naked body on social media. The truth is, for the first time in my life, I really saw myself as physically beautiful and sexually attractive in my own power, outside of men. I had never experienced so much turmoil in my friendships with women in all my years of living. I also had very close friend-ships take a step back from me after they said their piece, of course, because apparently, the pain of what I was walking through was too much for them to watch me go through. Emma was my very good friend, and I heard less and less from her when she got ill. She never allowed me to visit her; I was grieved but understood. Outside of Emma, at the beginning of my trial, I had friends who stayed neutral and so-called friends who tried to sabotage my character. But still, I pressed on because I knew inside no matter how crazy my life looked to others, I had to move forward because it didn't look crazy to me.

As far as counsel was concerned, I also had those who blamed me for my calamity. I had an ex-boyfriend tell me the reason everything was happening to me was that this was my karma. He would badmouth me to his friends, and the information would get back to me. He would be deceitful in financial dealings with me. When all this happened, I was in a place where he had the upper hand in my life. I was living with him and, in some ways, dependent, or else I would have been homeless. At the same time, I had friends telling me I needed to get out of the situation but provided no solutions or support. I moved out eventually, which I will go into later, and then made other decisions that seemed like mid-life crisis decisions. Later in my trial, when I took a leap of faith and journeyed to Alabama, my friends and some family looked at me like I was crazy. When I eventually had to return home, some said, "I told you so," while other close family members harbored resentment for me leaving in the first place. I was not only blamed for my financial woes but theirs as well. Imagine how horrible I felt and how I had to push to move through those emotions. But in all that, I kept my faith still.

Perhaps I was a lot like Job during that time. I know I tend to be very stubborn. Friends were giving me counsel, and I know there were times when I felt justified in my good or bad behavior. That's possibly why I understand Job. When hard-hitting information is being thrown at you in an intervention style, it's hard NOT to try to defend yourself and feel justified. No one wants to take a hard look in the mirror to make adjustments. Everything his friends told him he already knew, which tells me he was already taking a hard look at himself in the best possible way he knew how. Yet, he still had no understanding up till now. But just like any trial has a beginning, it eventually has to come to an end. Thank God for Job that the next voice that spoke to him came from a place of wisdom. Even in Job's frustration, he was smart enough and open to listen to that voice. That wisdom that Job listened to came in the form of another friend, which he least expected, who was also there silently waiting. More importantly, Job also heard the wisdom of God on the matter. Who better to speak to Job and about Job than the God within? Let's explore what happens next.

6

WHEN WISDOM SPEAKS

The Bible says that wisdom is the principal thing and that you should obtain it. And with all the wisdom you get, you should also obtain understanding. That tells me you can obtain wisdom and not understanding. It happens all the time in life. We are constantly given information that will enhance our lives, but if we don't take it in and take action, how does it benefit us? Our innate desire is to learn; we love obtaining knowledge—we were designed that way. But what do we do with the lessons we learn? Understanding gives you the tools to take action on the life lessons. That's why some of us repeat the same lessons; we have wisdom with no understanding. A child quickly understands that if they put their hand on a hot stove, they will get burnt. And so we need to take in the understanding of life's lessons.

When wisdom speaks to us, what does it sound like? For me, it's a beautiful voice that often breaks it down to me so eloquently. Other times, wisdom screams at me, especially when I haven't learned the lesson. The key is to get quiet and allow wisdom to speak. Two people can't have a civil conversation when both speak simultaneously: that's confusion. So, someone or something must be quiet, and usually, wisdom is smart enough to not say a word until you are finished talking. Wisdom is a gentleman like that. Once you're done and at a loss for words, wisdom steps in as the voice of reason. Job also had a time when wisdom began to speak to him as well. As you recall, when we left off, his three friends got so frustrated with him that they refused to talk again. They were done, which was good because what they brought had no value. Wisdom began speaking to Job in the most unusual way through an unexpected friend. As we pick up in Chapter 32, let's see how this unfolds:

> *1 So these three men ceased to answer Job,*
> *because he was righteous in his own eyes.*
> *2 Then was kindled the wrath of Elihu the son of*
> *Barachel the Buzite, of the kindred of Ram:*
> *against Job was his wrath kindled, because he*
> *justified himself rather than God.*
> *3 Also against his three friends was his wrath*
> *kindled, because they had found no answer,*
> *and yet had condemned Job.*
> *4 Now Elihu had waited till Job had spoken,*
> *because they were elder than he.*
> *5 When Elihu saw that there was no answer in*
> *the mouth of these three men, then his wrath*
> *was kindled.*

First of all, who was Elihu? The Bible mentions his lineage as the kindred of Ram. In the Bible, the spiritual meaning of Ram is wisdom and discernment. Go figure. In the Hebrew Bible, Ram was Hezron's son and an ancestor of David. This is important because David, in the Bible, was a great king. He was also known as a "man after God's own heart," and a figure loved among Christians. This same man was not perfect; as a matter of fact, he sent a man to war to be killed just so he could sleep with his wife. And this was God's man. I said earlier: God chooses whom he chooses, and the world's resume doesn't matter. God looks at the heart, and those who have the heart to answer His call will be used by Him.

So, Elihu, who was part of the lineage of wisdom, had some things he needed to say. Notice that the Bible says Elihu was equally angry with Job and his friends. He mentioned Job first, and I believe it's because he watched how Job responded to the foolishness disguised as counsel presented to Job by his friends. Have you ever watched someone in defense mode before? Have you ever thought to yourself, why are they responding that way? That's probably how Elihu felt. Let me give you an example, and of course, I'll use myself because I am not ashamed. The social media world can be treacherous at times. With me writing erotica, a lot of my social media content is very sensual. When I post a picture or reel, I can get a lot of hateful comments from those with no understanding of what I do or who I truly am. In my earlier years on the journey, I would find myself arguing and defending myself in the comments of my own content. Sometimes, the arguments got so heated that I would get blocked and reported by the person. Some days, the banter would go back and forth for hours.

I felt justified in my actions at the time because it was my page, and I felt like I was living life on my terms. Looking back on it now, I realize it was a senseless use of my time. I could have been doing other things to propel my life forward. It took wisdom and understanding for me to get there.

But just like wisdom, Elihu also waited for a couple of reasons. The first was out of respect for Job's age and his friends. The natural assumption is that the older, the wiser. Elihu perhaps was looking for some insight from Job's friends as well. As a matter of fact, he probably expected it. Imagine the letdown Elihu felt when Job's friends provided no solutions. Elihu had no choice but to speak up because, in an intervention, everyone has an opportunity to speak. As we jump to verses six through ten, it will shed some insight as to why wisdom was now saying:

> 6 And Elihu the son of Barachel the Buzite
>   answered and said, 'I am young, and ye are
>   very old; wherefore I was afraid, and durst
>   not show you mine opinion.
> 7 I said, Days should speak, and multitude of
>   years should teach wisdom.
> 8 But there is a spirit in man: and the inspiration
>   of the Almighty giveth them understanding.
> 9 Great men are not always wise: neither do the
>   aged understand judgment.
> 10 Therefore I said, Hearken to me; I also will
>   show mine opinion.

Elihu points out that he is much younger than Job and his counsel. Elihu had a lot he wanted to say, but he was afraid to speak because he was much younger. Elihu also wanted to be respectful and let age speak first because the assumption is that with age comes wisdom. Elihu found out firsthand that was not the case. How many of us can relate to that? How many of us have dismissed the counsel of others because they were younger than us? The truth is that many of my closest friends today are a little younger than me. I'm also a person that young people, in general, are drawn to. It could be because I listen to them with an open mind to understand how they think and feel; I actually listen to them. You must be open to wisdom in any form that comes to you because wisdom can speak in many ways.

Before Elihu even spoke, he got quiet. In silence is where wisdom lies. His silence gave him time to take in all the information that Job and his friends presented. Elihu listened with the intent to understand before he spoke. If we were honest with ourselves, most of the time, we, as people, often listen with the intent to formulate a rebuttal. We gather information as if we're in a debate, waiting for our opponent to finish their statement. Then, we jump right in with our argument. If you don't believe me, look at any marriage; spouses do it all the time, hence arguments. However, even in his youth, Elihu was wise enough to know that getting quiet was the key to hearing God's wisdom. It makes me wonder who was in HIS inner circle.

"There is a spirit in man..." when I read those words, the best version of myself seemed to leap within me. It tells me that the spirit of God lives in us all. We are connected to God. This infinite intelligence that lives within us gives us an understanding of everything. There is a solution for every challenge, which can only come from within. Elihu knew that deep within, he walked with God. I can only speculate here, but Elihu probably practiced a lifestyle of being quiet first. Elihu respected his elders. He valued their opinion. As a matter of fact, Elihu was waiting to hear wisdom from Job's core three in the hopes of obtaining knowledge for himself. When the wisdom of God could not express itself through Job's friends, it had to move on to someone who could listen, who was already quiet. The God within knew what Job needed, and the God within responded through the mouth of Elihu. The next part of the verse says, "and the inspiration of the Almighty giveth them understanding." Elihu also knew that whatever he was going to say to Job was going to be God-inspired. Once Elihu spoke, he expected Job's eyes of understanding to be opened. He wanted Job to be enlightened, but more than anything, Elihu wanted Job to be encouraged. Elihu was a true friend and good counsel to Job. Watch what happens in Chapter 32 when Elihu asks them to hear what he says. Let's begin with verse eleven:

> 11 Behold, I waited for your words; I gave ear to
>   your reasons, whilst ye searched out what
>   to say.
> 12 Yea, I attended unto you, and, behold, there
>   was none of you that convinced Job, or that
>   answered his words:
> 13 Lest ye should say, We have found out wisdom:
>   God thrusteth him down, not man.
> 14 Now he hath not directed his words against
>   me: neither will I answer him with your
>   speeches.
> 15 They were amazed, they answered no more:
>   they left off speaking.

Again, Elihu mentioned he waited to speak before sharing his thoughts. What surprises me is that Elihu mirrored Job's words to his friends: Your words provided no solutions, comfort, or value. Why were they amazed? I believe the amazement was not reverence for his profound wisdom, but that Elihu called them out on their actions. What could they really say? It was good that they were at a loss for words because Elihu said something significant before he even shared his opinion about what was happening to Job. Let's jump down to verse twenty in the same chapter:

> 20 *I will speak, that I may be refreshed: I will open my lips and answer.*
> 21 *Let me not, I pray you, accept any man's person, neither let me give flattering titles unto man.*
> 22 *For I know not to give flattering titles; in so doing my maker would soon take me away.*

Chapter 33:1-4 continues to say:

> 1 *Wherefore, Job, I pray thee, hear my speeches, and hearken to all my words.*
> 2 *Behold, now I have opened my mouth, my tongue hath spoken in my mouth.*
> 3 *My words shall be of the uprightness of my heart: and my lips shall utter knowledge clearly.*
> 4 *The spirit of God hath made me, and the breath of the Almighty hath given me life.*

Before Elihu provided his insight on the matter, he prayed. His prayer was simple: don't let me say what Job wants to hear, but what needs to be said. Elihu also humbled himself in prayer, acknowledging that any solutions provided would not come from him but from God. Elihu realized he was just the vessel to be used, and he prayed that his heart was pure and upright in delivering the message. Do you see the difference between Elihu and the others? The three musketeers came together and waited to express themselves without understanding or concern for what Job was going through. Did we see anywhere previously where any of them asked that God would humble them before they spoke? Did they ask God for insight into Job? Yes, they all acknowledged what they knew about God, but did they actually acknowledge God himself in their counsel? Elihu also prayed for his friend Job. Read chapters 32 and 33, and you will see this. They say prayer changes things, and I'm sure Job felt comfort from Elihu's words of prayer. If used properly, prayer is one of the most simple and powerful tools to move things forward. Yes, Job had been praying. He lived a life of religious practices. But sometimes, as humans, we really need and benefit from the prayers of those close to us who love us. Have you ever been in a place of hopelessness, and someone prayed for and with you? Sometimes, when others pray with you, they can say things that you don't know to say. Prayer from loved ones also lets you know they care about you and what you're going through. Prayer moves the mountains of our circumstances as we connect to the source of our being and find the solutions to peace in our lives. Knowing all this, why didn't Job's core three think to pray with him? They were religious, just like Job, so I'm sure they understood the power of prayer. They prayed among themselves before they got there, but not with him. Again, I believe their meeting with Job was an intervention. They were there to help him get his life back on course, or so they thought. They had no interest in praying with Job; their only interest was ensuring their friend got his life right with God.

Elihu shared his wisdom in the book of Job from chapters 33 to 38. There is so much in the text that I challenge you to read it for yourself; however, I will summarize my thoughts on what Elihu was saying to Job and his friends. First, we know that he was upset with Job and his friends. He was upset with Job because he felt justified in his actions and everything happening to him. He was more upset with Job's friends because they offered him no solutions but yet condemned him. We all have had people like that in our lives. Sometimes, their advice is unsolicited. If you love someone close to you, please don't offer advice if you have no real solutions.

One significant thing Elihu did that the others didn't do was acknowledge Job and what he was going through. He told him he was flesh and blood, just like him. See, the things Job went through can happen to us all at any given time. Most of us have lost loved ones, family members, our livelihood, and such. We all hit rock bottom because God is no respecter of persons. No one in this human suit is greater than the other or exempt from trials. The greater the trial, sometimes the greater your capacity to handle things. Elihu wanted Job to know that just like he went through hell and back, we all will have to take that journey at some point in this thing we call life.

Elihu also pointed out that God is still greater than man. He tells Job that God has been speaking this whole time. Chapter 33:12-17 says:

> 12 Behold, in this thou art not just: I will answer
>   thee, that God is greater than man.
> 13 Why dost thou strive against him? for he
>   giveth not account of any of his matters.

> *14 For God speaketh once, yea twice, yet man*
> *perceiveth it not.*
> *15 In a dream, in a vision of the night, when deep*
> *sleep falleth upon men, in slumberings upon*
> *the bed;*
> *16 Then he openeth the ears of men, and sealeth*
> *their instruction,*
> *17 That he may withdraw man from his purpose,*
> *and hide pride from man.*

God is greater than man, and he is always speaking. Even in your deepest despair, God is speaking, although it may seem you can't hear him. What do you do when you feel like God isn't speaking? Go to sleep. The text above from Job's wise friend indicates that God can download the answers to life's problems to us when a man sleeps. I personally believe this to be true. Not only because the Bible says so, but I believe that when we sleep, our souls leave our bodies, and we reconnect our souls to God for our answers. What do you think our soul does the whole time we're sleeping? Do you think it just sits there and watches your body sleep? Absolutely not! Your soul is immortal, so it's always looking for versions of the best you. In this human suit, we are subject to everything in our environment that is a buffer to the source of it all. Our work, families, and where we live take our focus off what we truly came here to do. But when we sleep, we have a clear path to the source, the all-knowing and powerful.

There is something to be said about getting proper rest. Doctors stress it all the time. Why do you think that is? If adequate rest is essential for your physical well-being, why wouldn't it benefit your spiritual well-being? The natural world is purely a replica of things in the spiritual world, so what we do to enhance our lives physically can also impact our spirituality. Getting proper rest rejuvenates the body. But now we also know that God gives us life instructions when we sleep. If you're feeling depressed, sleep a little more. Scholars will probably disagree, but if God's answers are in the night when we can't interject our own ideas and opinions, then wouldn't the answers to getting out of depression be there as well? Just a thought.

Elihu also encouraged Job. He let Job know that God will never leave you in what feels like the valley of despair. Take a look at Chapter 33:23:

> *23 If there be a messenger with him, an inter-*
> *preter, one among a thousand, to show unto*
> *man his uprightness.*

He also says he is not trying to understand why God allows things to happen as they do, but his purpose is in everything. Chapter 33:29-31:

> *29 Lo, all these things worketh God oftentimes*
> *with man,*
> *30 To bring back his soul from the pit, to be*
> *enlightened with the light of the living.*
> *31 Mark well, O Job, hearken unto me: hold thy*
> *peace, and I will speak.*

From this text, I understand that there is a lesson in everything we experience. We come through the valley of despair in a situation with insight that we didn't have before. Once again, I'll use my life experience as an example. I don't mind being the sacrificial lamb. When I was in a relationship with my hot young ex, it started out steamy. When things are hot like that, you tend to ignore the red flags sitting right in front of you. It wasn't until after we broke up and moved into a somewhat poly situation that I began to see him for who he truly was. Everything is a learning experience, and there is a purpose for everything we go through.

I want to take a side note here and talk about purpose. Purpose is not this big mysterious word or state of being. Purpose simply is. It is who you are, what you came to do, and the experiences you and God decided you would take on. No one human being's life purpose is greater than the next. On that note, don't ever judge why someone came into existence and who they are. You don't know who they are and what they are called to be. When you judge, you go strictly by what you see. People go through bad things and fall on hard times. It's all for our greater purpose. What I came in this lifetime to do and what you came to do are different. I'm often suspicious of folks who judge others when they see them at their worst. Hell, some folks judge even when people are doing their best. The Bible says not to judge unless you want to be judged. Be careful what you say about others because those fingers will point right back at you. The greatest, most successful people have been through trials you couldn't imagine.

Some faced homelessness, sexual assault, loss of limbs, etc., only to rise above it all to be the greatest version of themselves. That is purpose, that is simply being. The problem is we want to live this fantastic life of purpose, but we don't want to walk through what it takes to get there. Walking in purpose and what you believe you are called to do will be uncomfortable; it will be painful, and there is no way around that. Study any successful person, and I can assure you that their story will be full of trials, failures, and setbacks that led them to the path they are on today. If you are living, you have a purpose. It's okay to feel pain, hurt, and failure. All these things are just par for the course of life.

Elihu asked Job to respectfully remain silent while he turned the conversation to his friends, the three "wise men," in Chapter 34:

> *1 Furthermore, Elihu answered and said,*
> *2 Hear my words, O ye wise men; and give ear*
>   *unto me, ye that have knowledge.*
> *3 For the ear trieth words, as the mouth tasteth*
>   *meat.*
> *4 Let us choose to us judgment: let us know*
>   *among ourselves what is good.*
> *5 For Job hath said, I am righteous: and God hath*
>   *taken away my judgment.*
> *6 Should I lie against my right? My wound is*
>   *incurable without transgression.*
> *7 What man is like Job, who drinketh up scorning*
>   *like water?*
> *8 Which goeth in company with the workers of*
>   *iniquity, and walketh with wicked men.*
> *9 For he hath said, It profiteth a man nothing*
>   *that he should delight himself with God.*
> *10 Therefore hearken unto me, ye men of under-*
>   *standing: far be it from God, that he should do*
>   *wickedness; and from the Almighty, that he*
>   *should commit iniquity.*
> *11 For the work of a man shall he render unto*

> *him, and cause every man to find according to*
>   *his ways.*
> *12 Yea, surely God will not do wickedly, neither*
>   *will the Almighty pervert judgment.*
> *13 Who hath given him a charge over the earth?*
>   *or who hath disposed the whole world?*
> *14 If he set his heart upon man, if he gather unto*
>   *himself his spirit and his breath;*
> *15 All flesh shall perish together, and man shall*
>   *turn again unto dust.*
> *16 If now thou hast understanding, hear this:*
>   *hearken to the voice of my words.*
> *17 Shall even he that hateth right govern? and*
>   *wilt thou condemn him that is most just?*
> *18 Is it fit to say to a king, Thou art wicked? and*
>   *to princes, Ye are ungodly?*
> *19 How much less to him that accepteth not the*
>   *persons of princes, nor regardeth the rich*
>   *more than the poor? for they all are the work*
>   *of his hands.*

I thought it was significant to include all this text because there is so much Elihu had to say to Job's counsel of friends. His first question to them was who they were to judge Job's righteousness. Instead of his friends looking at Job as a pillar of strength, they immediately went into judging Job because they could only see his external environment. Elihu challenged them to marvel at his strength, his capacity to still love and trust the unknown source despite what was happening. Elihu said, "What man is like Job, who drinks scorning like water?" What I believe he means is I am truly in awe of what this man has gone through and can still look deep within to God for the answers. It was truly marvelous in his eyes. You see, sometimes, when all hell breaks loose in our lives, and we handle it with surrender to those on the outside looking in, we make it look a little easy.

They marvel because they cannot imagine being able to walk through what YOU have been through. And then there are those like the three wise men who look at your trial and feel they could handle it better than you. I can say this statement is true from firsthand experience. I had my first son, Aaron, at the age of 15. I'll tell that whole story in another book. Still, by the time Aaron was almost 3, I noticed he was starting to regress mentally. Small words that he learned he stopped saying; he would spend lots of time alone, and he really wasn't around a lot of children, considering I was a teenage mother who only worked and went to school. Aaron began to act out and throw tantrums instead of using his words to get what he wanted. He stayed up most days until about 3 a.m. and would wake back up around 7. Aaron would damage the walls when he threw tantrums and tried to hit himself or others in frustration. But not in a menacing way. When I was raising Aaron from ages 3 to 8, I mostly received responses from others about how terrible a child he was. No one understood what was wrong with him, and honestly, there weren't many people who had the time to really care about my life at that time.

When I say that, I mean this: some of my strongest support people were fighting their own demons. We were fighting homelessness, addictions, and family traumas in our household, so the primary focus of my mother and siblings was not getting help for Aaron. It was on survival. Well, around 7, that help came from my sister. She was taking a psychology course and had to do a research paper on autism. Remember that this is back in the early 90s when information was beginning to become available. My sister had to go into the home of a family who was raising a young boy with autism. She noticed the familiarity between him and Aaron and encouraged me to do research. I did, and shortly after that, he received the diagnosis that I knew to be true. There were people in my life who now understood. Their thinking was transformed because they now had understanding. This led to more compassion and then marvel. And that is the point Elihu was trying to make to Job's magnificent counsel.

He also reminds Job's friends that God doesn't favor one person over another. If you continue to read in this chapter, Elihu also reminds them that God sees everything. Can you imagine God sees everything about us, our thoughts, dreams, and desires? Most of us immediately go to all the bad things we've done when we think about a big God, the Source of it all, Infinite Intelligence paying attention to our every move. But that's not how God sees us. God is not looking for the bad that we do because God is good. He doesn't look down to see judgment; he sees love. When you feel love, God's connection is looking at you. God looks at us and sees success; he sees victory. God looks at us in pride and adoring love like a parent looks at a child who takes their first steps. That is God. That is love.

At the end of Chapter 34, Elihu sums up what he wants to say to Job's wise counsel by telling them to speak about the things they genuinely know about in verse 33:

> 33 Should it be according to thy mind? he will
>   recompense it, whether thou refuse, or
>   whether thou choose; and not I: therefore
>   speak what thou knowest.

> *34 Let men of understanding tell me, and let a*
>   *wise man hearken unto me.*

I could expound on that, but it seems pretty easy to comprehend, wouldn't you agree? Elihu is saying that if you really don't know the depth of what Job has gone through firsthand, and if you're not God, you should sit this one out. But Elihu was not finished, as he turned his attention back to Job in this same Chapter in the very following verses:

> *35 Job hath spoken without knowledge, and his*
>   *words were without wisdom.*
> *36 My desire is that Job may be tried unto the end*
>   *because of his answers for wicked men.*

Elihu wanted Job to acknowledge that he had allowed his emotions and feelings to get the best of him in this intervention. Chapter 35 focuses on how Job needed to be accountable for his words. Elihu pointed out that Job spoke out of turn because he felt justified in his circumstances. Job was in victim mode for those seven-plus days, asking, "Why me?" Please don't judge Job harshly; we have all been in this place. When we focus on the 'why' from a place of desperation, it's hard to hear that inner voice we call God. Why? Because God is not there. God's nature is not desperation, fear, worry, or anxiety. Unanswered prayers live in the land of desperation; God does not hear prayers of desperation, need, and lack. This may be tough for many to believe because some of you visualize God as a slave master that you must beg for a crust of bread and then cry with gratitude. After all, you believe that is all you deserve. That is not the God who loves us.

If you don't believe what I'm saying, think about your own life. If you have children or a significant other, how do you see them? Don't you love them and want to give them the world to the best of your capacity? Do you hear them when they are selfish, angry, and refuse to listen? Do you rush in to give them the extras? Absolutely not! What about a desperate lover who is needy? When they want to dominate your time, energy, and money, do you willingly participate in that one-sided relationship? So why do we think the great I AM, the creator of the universe, would want to be in the presence of that type of behavior? If we are made in the image of God, and God does not respond to desperation, unworthiness, victimization, and the like. Then, we should avoid those behaviors as well. After all, aren't we connected to God? If you believe that is true, then you have the power within you to change from within.

Elihu wanted Job and his friends to know that God could pull them out no matter the trial if they got quiet and heard His voice. Let's look at Chapter 36:10-12:

> 10 He openeth also their ear to discipline, and
>   commandeth that they return from iniquity.
> 11 If they obey and serve him, they shall spend
>   their days in prosperity, and their years in
>   pleasures.
> 12 But if they obey not, they shall perish by the
>   sword, and they shall die without knowledge.

Elihu highlights what God is saying. When we see the words "return from iniquity," we immediately think of some deadly sin we have been involved in. That's a fear-based thought, and God doesn't operate in fear. Turning away from iniquity is simply making a change. We have all heard the saying that the definition of insanity is doing the same thing over and over and expecting a different result; well, making a change involves doing something different. If you're miserable at your job, you may have to go within and ask yourself what's next. If you're facing a divorce, you must decide if you want to fight for your marriage. Whatever is not working in your life, go within and acknowledge it and God, and make the changes you need to. It's way too easy to do but also difficult because people generally don't want to come face to face with the person who is truly the source of all the chaos in their lives, which is themselves. It's easy not to acknowledge that. But when you do, you tap into God, and your life begins to change day by day. Every day, you become new. However, if you refuse to acknowledge that you created the mess that has become your life. Then, the changes you desire will never occur. All those hopes, dreams, and goals that you have for your life will die with you if you refuse to make changes.

Finally, Elihu ended what he needed to say to them in a magnificent way. In the same chapter, Chapter 36, verse 26, Elihu begins to describe the magnificence of God:

> 26 Behold, God is great, and we know him not,
>   neither can the number of his years be
>   searched out.
> 27 For he maketh small the drops of water: they
>   pour down rain according to the vapour
>   thereof:
> 28 Which the clouds do drop and distil upon man
>   abundantly.

> *29 Also, can any understand the spreadings of the clouds, or the noise of his tabernacle?*
> *30 Behold, he spreadeth his light upon it, and covereth the bottom of the sea.*
> *31 For by them judgeth he the people; he giveth meat in abundance.*

In Chapter 37, he continues:

> *1 At this also my heart trembleth, and is moved out of his place.*
> *2 Hear attentively the noise of his voice, and the sound that goeth out of his mouth.*
> *3 He directeth it under the whole heaven, and his lightning unto the ends of the earth.*
> *4 After it a voice roareth: he thundereth with the voice of his excellency; and he will not stay them when his voice is heard.*
> *5 God thundereth marvellously with his voice; great things doeth he, which we cannot comprehend.*

Elihu wants Job and his companions to know that they can't even begin to comprehend how big God is. The three wise men had reduced God to their own personal perceptions and reflected them onto Job. Job had his own perceptions of how God operated and thus had become stuck in religious acts. Yes, Job had gotten caught up in doing the routine so much that he forgot about the intention behind why he conducted his everyday affairs. Job's relationship with God and himself had become routine. Elihu also challenged them to look around at the earth's vastness and look at nature. He then goes on to describe the beautiful things in nature in such detail. Elihu talks about everyday things that we stop noticing that remain in order because of a great God. Go back and read the whole Chapter for yourself. Better yet, pondering the vastness of an infinite being is as simple as looking out your window. I look at the tall trees, and there are plenty of them. The birds that wake us up in the morning with the sound of their beautiful voices. Butterflies in the summer and fresh soft grass that feels good on your bare feet. Even those small things in our own world reflect how big God truly is. Take a minute to pause and think about that.

I believe Elihu was excited at this point! How could you not be when you reflect on the goodness of God? Reflecting on God's goodness does not have to be some religious practice, which, unfortunately, we have made it to be. We religiously pray and walk away, thinking we have accomplished something. I'll touch on that in the next chapter, but when you appreciate the little things, you send a vibration of gratitude to the one who created you. Gratitude gets God's attention. In Elihu's excitement, he asked Job, "Do you know when God formed all this?" and pointed out God's excellency and justness. Go back and read it for yourself. Elihu went on for a chapter and a half about the wonder and amazement that we call God through all that he has created. Oh, he was detailed in his gratitude; he didn't just say God made the trees and the pigs; he was in awe of God's specificity of his creation and the intention behind all that he created, including you and me. And then what happens next? Let's take a look at Chapter 38, verse 1:

> *1 Then the Lord answered Job out of the whirlwind, and said,*

God immediately showed up... Once Elihu entered into a state of gratitude, God showed up. We all know things are about to change when times are tough, and God steps on the scene. Change can be exciting but can also be painful. Why? Because there is no one to contend with but God and you. But the good news is that growth and beauty are on the other side of dealing with you. What did God have to say to Job? A whole lot, and we'll dissect that together in the next chapter.

7

WHEN GOD SPEAKS

I n this final chapter, we will address what happens when God intervenes. The final chapters of Job address God speaking primarily and then what happens to Job next. What I find interesting is that God speaks in less than three full chapters. In contrast, Job's contention with his friends occupies most of the book of Job, as I previously mentioned. I wonder why that is. It could be because God simply is, and there wasn't anything that God spoke that could be disputed. Or it could be that God didn't need to say as much as Job's counsel. Whatever the case, God spoke, and it was powerful. As I was writing this chapter, a part of me wanted to gloss over it because I was very familiar with the story of Job. However, after reading these last two chapters, I struggled with organizing the material because there was so much that God was revealing to me through the text. To make this book make sense to the reader and myself, I'll go through the final chapters, give my interpretation, and then give my thoughts on the lessons that Job learned from going through all of this. Again, this is my interpretation, so take what resonates and leave the rest behind for someone else. I'll also share my personal story of how I came to myself and saw an open door to the end of what I was going through. May this final chapter and the dialogue between God and Job give you insight into your own journey.

When we left off, God began to speak. Let's look at Chapter 38, verse 1 again:

> 1 Then the Lord answered Job out of the whirl-
>   wind, and said,

Pause. It says the Lord answered Job and said...but wasn't Elihu speaking? Elihu was engulfed in the praise and wonder of God, remember. Elihu was talking to Job about God's wonder, so why would God show up and answer Job? This also leads me to question how God spoke to Job and HOW he showed up. When God speaks to us, God does not show up as a white man with a beard or a black man with dreads; God shows up and speaks, and you KNOW that it is God. Where does God speak? Usually in our mind and heart. So, as Elihu was in marvelous praise of the master of the universe, God showed up to address Job based on what was going on in his mind and heart. What was going on in Job's mind and heart? We can speculate as to what was happening, but verses 2 and 3 give us an indicator:

> 2 Who is this that darkeneth counsel by words
>   without knowledge?
> 3 Gird up now thy loins like a man; for I will
>   demand of thee, and answer thou me.

God always asks questions that He already knows the answers to. I also believe Job knew that, too! He got Job's attention by telling him whatever you're thinking will destroy you in the end. Before God would allow Job to continue in his own self-pity of thoughts, He had to step in. God then asks Job one question in an elaborate way, "Where were YOU when all this was created?" If you don't believe me, let's examine Chapter 38 together, starting with verse 4:

> *4 Where wast thou when I laid the foundations of the earth? declare, if thou hast understanding.*
>
> *5 Who hath laid the measures thereof, if thou knowest? or who hath stretched the line upon it?*
>
> *6 Whereupon are the foundations thereof fastened? or who laid the cornerstone thereof;*
>
> *7 When the morning stars sang together, and all the sons of God shouted for joy?*
>
> *8 Or who shut up the sea with doors, when it brake forth, as if it had issued out of the womb?*
>
> *9 When I made the cloud the garment thereof, and thick darkness a swaddling band for it,*
>
> *10 And brake up for it my decreed place, and set bars and doors,*
>
> *11 And said, Hitherto shalt thou come, but no further: and here shall thy proud waves be stayed?*
>
> *12 Hast thou commanded the morning since thy days; and caused the dayspring to know his place;*
>
> *13 That it might take hold of the ends of the earth, that the wicked might be shaken out of it?*

14 *It is turned as clay to the seal; and they stand as a garment.*

15 *And from the wicked their light is withholden, and the high arm shall be broken.*

16 *Hast thou entered into the springs of the sea? or hast thou walked in the search of the depth?*

17 *Have the gates of death been opened unto thee? or hast thou seen the doors of the shadow of death?*

18 *Hast thou perceived the breadth of the earth? declare if thou knowest it all.*

19 *Where is the way where light dwelleth? and as for darkness, where is the place thereof,*

20 *That thou shouldest take it to the bound thereof, and that thou shouldest know the paths to the house thereof?*

21 *Knowest thou it, because thou wast then born? or because the number of thy days is great?*

22 *Hast thou entered into the treasures of the snow? or hast thou seen the treasures of the hail,*

23 *Which I have reserved against the time of trouble, against the day of battle and war?*

24 *By what way is the light parted, which scattereth the east wind upon the earth?*

25 *Who hath divided a watercourse for the overflowing of waters, or a way for the lightning of thunder;*

26 *To cause it to rain on the earth, where no man is; on the wilderness, wherein there is no man;*

27 *To satisfy the desolate and waste ground; and*

to cause the bud of the tender herb to spring
forth?

28 Hath the rain a father? or who hath begotten
the drops of dew?

29 Out of whose womb came the ice? and the
hoary frost of heaven, who hath gendered it?

30 The waters are hid as with a stone, and the
face of the deep is frozen.

31 Canst thou bind the sweet influences of
Pleiades, or loose the bands of Orion?

32 Canst thou bring forth Mazzaroth in his
season? or canst thou guide Arcturus with his
sons?

33 Knowest thou the ordinances of heaven? canst
thou set the dominion thereof in the earth?

34 Canst thou lift up thy voice to the clouds, that
abundance of waters may cover thee?

35 Canst thou send lightnings, that they may go
and say unto thee, Here we are?

36 Who hath put wisdom in the inward parts? or
who hath given understanding to the heart?

37 Who can number the clouds in wisdom? or
who can stay the bottles of heaven,

38 When the dust groweth into hardness, and the
clods cleave fast together?

39 Wilt thou hunt the prey for the lion? or fill the
appetite of the young lions,

40 When they couch in their dens, and abide in
the covert to lie in wait?

41 Who provideth for the raven his food? when
his young ones cry unto God, they wander for
lack of meat.

As you can see, God goes into explicit detail about His creation. He can do that because He created it. Consider this: as a writer of short stories, those stories are embedded in me because I created them. All creation belongs to God, so God would be detailed when He speaks. God was not speaking about the things created just to be talking. God is very specific. There was a reason Elihu turned their attention to creation before God came on the scene. God wants us to pay attention to creation for several reasons. The first is that we have the power within us to create. If you don't believe me, look around your room. You created the bed you wanted to sleep in, the pictures on your wall, and the phone you choose to look at every morning as soon as you open your eyes. That's your world; you created that. I also believe God wants us to know that whatever He creates can be abundant. There are no shortages of oceans, animals, human beings, or even fruits and vegetables. In fact, all those things continue to multiply. God wanted Job to remember the realization of who he truly was. God talked about laying the foundations of the earth, aligning the stars and the galaxies, and creating life. But God did not stop there. He had to manage the oceans and seas, keep the planets aligned, and ensure that all the living things He created, including you and me, were provided for.

In chapters 38 and 39, God describes the timing of things set forth in creation. God reminds Job that I Am is creation and asks where he was when light was created. A lot was said in these two chapters, and God was showing Job how marvelous He is through creation. When we think about everyday creation around us, when we tune in, we have no choice but to recognize that someone or something bigger than us was responsible for this. God described supposedly mystical creatures such as the unicorn, so they must exist (Chap. 39:10). This tells me that any creature we deem mystical, even what we call extra-terrestrials, do exist. We as humans would be foolish to believe that we are the only or even the most intelligent beings in the galaxy. To do so would limit God in who He is and how He expresses Himself. But God was not finished. God and Job dialogued in Chapter 40, verses 1-7:

> *1 Moreover, the Lord answered Job, and said,*
> *2 'Shall he that contendeth with the Almighty*
>   *instruct Him? He that reproveth God, let him*
>   *answer it.'*
> *3 Then Job answered the Lord, and said,*
> *4 'Behold, I am vile; what shall I answer thee? I*
>   *will lay mine hand upon my mouth.*
> *5 Once have I spoken; but I will not answer: yea,*
>   *twice; but I will proceed no further.'*
> *6 Then answered the Lord unto Job out of the*
>   *whirlwind, and said,*
> *7 'Gird up thy loins now like a man: I will*
>   *demand of thee, and declare thou unto me.*

God asks Job before he answers if he has the ability to give God direction and instruction. Essentially, He's saying, "Job, when did YOU become so all-knowing of things that you can instruct me on your life?" After everything I have shown you that I have set in creation, do you still hold to your own understanding? God didn't even describe a fraction of His creation in his conversation with Job. Yet, Job still had feelings of whatever he was feeling somewhere in his heart. I will not speculate what Job was thinking. Remember, God said twice to Job to provide an answer. The text doesn't indicate that Job said anything audibly. But since God is pure awareness, He was aware of the thoughts floating in Job's head and demanded Job be accountable for his thinking. Job's response was pure humility, and I love it!

To summarize, Job said, "God, you got me. You know and see everything. I've misspoken more than once. I'm smart enough to know when to shut my mouth and hear wisdom." In verses 6 and 7, we know that God is not finished with Job because He repeats Himself again and demands an answer from Job about the things He's about to speak upon in the following verses:

> 8 Wilt thou also disannul my judgment? Wilt
>   thou condemn me, that thou mayest be
>   righteous?
> 9 Hast thou an arm like God? Or canst thou
>   thunder with a voice like Him?
> 10 Deck thyself now with majesty and excellency;
>   and array thyself with glory and beauty."

These three verses are self-explanatory. He's asking Job, who do you really think you are to step into the role of God in your life? What I love about verse 10 is how God describes Himself in the text as glorious, beautiful, majestic, and excellent. Those are attributes of God. Essentially, as God is asking him if he is God, He's asking, "Do you have the capacity to not only set and keep creation in order but can you also radiate these attributes while doing so?" Deep, I know. Then God does what God does best, turns Job's attention back to creation. We go into Chapter 41 for this example, but I will take a few snippets from different verses to explain what God was saying here. Let's start with Chapter 41, verses 1-7:

> *1 Canst thou draw out leviathan with a hook? Or his tongue with a cord which thou lettest down?*
>
> *2 Canst thou put a hook into his nose? Or bore his jaw through with a thorn?*
>
> *3 Will he make many supplications unto thee? Will he speak soft words unto thee?*
>
> *4 Will he make a covenant with thee? Wilt thou take him for a servant forever?*
>
> *5 Wilt thou play with him as with a bird? Or wilt thou bind him for thy maidens?*
>
> *6 Shall the companions make a banquet of him? Shall they part him among the merchants?*
>
> *7 Canst thou fill his skin with barbed irons? Or his head with fish spears?*

Verse 11 goes on to say:

> *11 Who hath prevented me, that I should repay him? Whatsoever is under the whole heaven is mine.*

God wants to point out again that not only is He marvelous and majestic, but God is strong and powerful. In Chapter 40, God mentions the Behemoth and how even its strength doesn't compare to God. God also points out to Job that in the end, God decides what happens to the Leviathan, even in all its strength and might, and the Leviathan knows that. As a matter of fact, God is trying to get Job to understand that all creation knows what human beings seem to forget. That God is creation, and all creation belongs to God.

In this beautiful climax of the conversation, Job speaks again in the realization of who God truly is to him in Chapter 42. Like any movie, a climax indicates an emotionally charged conclusion or point that must be made. Let's see how the rest of this conversation unfolds in Chapter 42, verses 1-6:

> *1 Then Job answered the Lord, and said,*
> *2 'I know that thou canst do everything, and that*
> *no thought can be withheld from thee.*
> *3 Who is he that hideth counsel without knowl-*
> *edge? Therefore have I uttered that I under-*
> *stood not; things too wonderful for me, which*
> *I knew not.*
> *4 Hear, I beseech thee, and I will speak: I will*
> *demand of thee, and declare thou unto me.*
> *5 I have heard of thee by the hearing of the ear:*
> *but now mine eye seeth thee.*
> *6 Wherefore I abhor myself, and repent in dust*
> *and ashes.*

Job had the moment of truly coming to himself and realizing who God truly was, something so enormous that words can't even describe the magnificence of God, although the writer of this Chapter did an excellent job in the attempt. When you read these chapters, how can you not understand the bigness of God? Imagine being responsible for creating galaxies and ensuring that they continue to orbit. In addition, populating those galaxies with unique lifeforms and providing for them. And then there is little ole you that God must keep His watchful eye on. Could you really do that? I think not. Job realized that because his spiritual eyes were open to that reality. He acknowledged this to God and became a changed man. True repentance, as the religious folks say, goes beyond acknowledgment and becoming someone new. A change of heart is the only true change that takes place.

It was now time for God to turn His attention to Job's friends; remember them, the three wise men as I like to refer to them in jest? Well, God had something to say to them as well, and I was blown away when I read the next verses in Chapter 42:

> 7 *And it was so, that after the Lord had spoken these words unto Job, the Lord said to Eliphaz the Temanite, 'My wrath is kindled against thee, and against thy two friends: for ye have not spoken of me the thing that is right, as my servant Job hath.*
>
> 8 *Therefore take unto you now seven bullocks and seven rams, and go to my servant Job, and offer up for yourselves a burnt offering; and my servant Job shall pray for you: for him will I accept: lest I deal with you after your folly, in that ye have not spoken of me the thing which is right, like my servant Job.'*
>
> 9 *So Eliphaz the Temanite and Bildad the Shuhite and Zophar the Naamathite went, and did according as the Lord commanded them: the Lord also accepted Job.*

Now, let's break this down. First, God addressed Eliphaz. He did not speak to the other two specifically; why was that? Could it be because he was the first to address Job with his ideas of why this was happening to him? Maybe he spearheaded the whole intervention—who knows? But in some manner, Eliphaz was obviously the ringleader of the group, so God addressed him directly. He did not call the other two by name, which is very interesting. The requirement for burnt offerings to Job was telling because, again, burnt offerings are meant for atonement, so they had to return humbly to Job. Imagine that.

God even let them know that this was the ONLY way He could accept their change of heart because if they came to Him in their current state, God would have no choice but to let the laws that He set in order deal with them. God does not overstep His own laws, which He put in place, no matter how nice you are or how close you think you are to God, through religious acts. What are these laws? Some call it the law of attraction, but it's way bigger than that. These men were operating in judgment, showed no empathy for Job's situation, and came off as if they were better than Job for what he was going through. The laws of God would have had no choice but to reflect those things back to those men in a more terrible way than Job experienced. Have you ever heard of a situation where someone has talked about another in judgment and found themselves facing the same type of situation? Why do you think there is a phrase that says, "never say never"? That phrase is a simple law; the Bible even says not to judge unless you want to be subject to that same judgment. I find it ironic that these men had to go through Job to get to God, which leads me to this point: God cannot and will not allow things such as pride, arrogance, fear, neediness, and, most of all, judgment to go unaccounted for in our lives if we want to grow into more of the attributes of God. Job's closest counsel was guilty mostly of judging Job when he was at his lowest, so for them to make amends, they had to go back to the source first and then, in humility, back to Job.

What I also love about this story is verse nine in this chapter:

> 9 *So Eliphaz the Temanite and Bildad the Shuhite*
> *and Zophar the Naamathite went, and did*
> *according as the Lord commanded them: the*
> *Lord also accepted Job.*

These men were smart enough to do what God asked of them, and their offering was accepted through Job. This tells me that their hearts were in a place where they could hear God and put themselves in a position to make changes. It also tells me that God loves them so much that He didn't want their behaviors to eventually destroy them. God knew that if they continued in judgment and self-righteousness, eventually, it would kill them. Our ego has no place in the beautiful things that God is. If you don't believe God wanted to preserve His creation, think about something you have created; I'll use children for this example. Sometimes, a child may do something so out of the ordinary in a negative way that we do not want to deal with the child at the moment. For example, a teenager getting caught stealing. As a parent, you're outraged by the behavior and can see where it could lead, so you make course corrections for your child in hopes that they will understand and adjust. As we all know, sometimes they do, and others don't. But the point is

God loved them still and wanted them to grow. Even Job's trial served as a lesson of growth for his friends; one cannot judge a situation based upon their own perception or how they believe they would have handled the situation better. I pray his three friends understood their lesson and grew from the situation. Unfortunately, the end of the story does not get that specific. I'll share the rest of the story, and then I'll share Job's lessons from my point of view, so take what resonates and leave the rest. Let's look at the end of Chapter 42, verses 10-17:

> *10 And the Lord turned the captivity of Job, when he prayed for his friends: also the Lord gave Job twice as much as he had before.*
>
> *11 Then came there unto him all his brethren, and all his sisters, and all they that had been of his acquaintance before, and did eat bread with him in his house: and they bemoaned him, and comforted him over all the evil that the Lord had brought upon him: every man also gave him a piece of money, and every one an earring of gold.*
>
> *12 So the Lord blessed the latter end of Job more than his beginning: for he had fourteen thousand sheep, and six thousand camels, and a thousand yoke of oxen, and a thousand she-asses.*
>
> *13 He had also seven sons and three daughters.*
>
> *14 And he called the name of the first, Jemima; and the name of the second, Kezia; and the name of the third, Keren-happuch.*
>
> *15 And in all the land were no women found so fair as the daughters of Job: and their father*

> *gave them an inheritance among their brethren.*
> *16 After this Job lived a hundred and forty years, and saw his sons, and his sons' sons, even four generations.*
> *17 So Job died, being old and full of days.*

Let's break all of this down. Job had compassion and love and prayed to God on behalf of his friends. After he did this, God gave him twice as much as he had before! There is something about praying and sending compassion for others, not only during the apparent hell you perceive that you're going through but also for the very ones he loved most who had judged him. For anyone, that's big, but guess what that is? Forgiveness. God is telling us that forgiveness will take us a whole lot further than holding on to the memories of judgment or any other past wrong that we may feel that another has done to us.

Verse 11 talks about how his family and friends all returned to him. Perhaps the three musketeers were there. Who knows because the scripture says all of his acquaintances. What I love is they ate with him, drank with him, and showed him love and compassion. What Job showed to his friends was returned to him, which is beautiful. Job got a whole new family, more children, land, massive wealth, and all of the above. Job lived the last days of his life greater than his beginning before all of this started. Of course, again, his latter days were a process of time. He had to remarry and have ten more children, and in that process, he gained all he did. I believe, however, that Job learned to enjoy the journey of the rest of his life, appreciating and realizing that everything we go through provides lessons we learn to make us better as human beings as a whole. Those lessons we learn act as roadmaps to guide us along our journey. Some of these lessons come from the places of our trials. Still, other lessons we learn can be from beautiful experiences, such as listening to a child's conversation. The key is to embrace the lessons that all of life seems to be trying to teach us. Job also realized everything he went through was well worth the ending.

8

THE LESSONS

Now that we have explored how this fascinating story unfolds, I'd like to share the lessons I gleaned from it. This perspective is my own, and I hope it will be helpful to those who read it. However, remember, I am neither God nor the creator of all, so take what you need from this to aid your journey. I believe Job learned extensively during his trial, primarily about himself, and anytime we undergo something, the lesson is for us—not to judge the situation or the people involved. Thus, I believe God was pleased. After all, God knew from the beginning what Job was made of, having created him. With that said, God knows exactly what you are made of, too. No person, place, or circumstance is intended to keep you down. Unlimited possibilities already reside within you. Let's delve into the lessons.

The first lesson Job learned was the realization that he alone had created the circumstances and trials he faced. The things he imagined and feared materialized into his reality. His worries about losing everything manifested into an actual physical reality. That's why it is crucial to be mindful of what you think, say, and listen to—whatever Job thought about appeared in his life in a terrifying form! Have you ever experienced this? I'm sure you have; we all have. The problem is that we often refuse to accept responsibility for the creation of our lives. You might blame your ex-spouse for a divorce, your boss for job dissatisfaction, and sometimes, even God for your troubles. However, we are the common denominator in our lives, so if we dislike what we see, we must acknowledge our role in its creation.

The next lesson Job learned was that he had outgrown his former self. He lost his family, possessions, health, and even his friends, who failed to recognize who he had become. Job realized he needed to evolve his thinking and behaviors. Considering who he surrounded himself with, he recognized that his friends knew even less about God than he did. Job needed to ascend to a spiritual counsel that could elevate his thinking to match his spiritual journey in later life. Though Job's heart was in the right place with his ritualistic practices, he deeply knew they were insufficient. Sometimes, going deeper requires losing everything—not necessarily materially. However, that can happen, but you must shed everything you've known about who you are, what you want, and what life means to you. This understanding led to another profound lesson. My journey taught me that sometimes, you must lose it all to let go of the rest.

Job had to learn the third and most powerful lesson: no matter how well-intentioned others are, you must find answers within yourself. Going within requires being in a place where you can hear what God is trying to tell you. I realize this sounds mysterious, and it appears impossible when you face what seems like hell. But with God, all things are possible. The issue is that we often expect God to speak in dramatic ways, as seen in movies. God speaks in every moment and action, and his communication can be very subtle. Another issue is our reluctance to do the internal work required. Why? Because it forces us to confront what's truly inside—our impatience, the people we refuse to forgive, and the dreams we've neglected to pursue. Who wants to face all that? Unfortunately, we must venture inward to reach the better side of our trials.

I'll share an example that illustrates this process, which God revealed to me during my experiences. One day, as I prepared a snack of watermelon, I thought about how perfectly I had cut the pieces and considered freezing them. Searching for a suitable plastic bowl for the freezer, I faced a disorganized cabinet filled with mismatched lids—a metaphor for the chaos in our lives. Initially, I considered blaming my daughter, who lived with me, for the mess. However, I realized that I had contributed to this chaos. Faced with the possibility that the matching lid might not even be there, I felt frustrated. It seemed easier to choose another bowl, but a part of me insisted on finding the lid for the one I had selected. As I organized the lids, shifting from frustration to focused action, I eventually found the unique, beautifully bright lid I was looking for. This simple act of organizing a cabinet mirrored the work we must continually do on ourselves—acknowledging and addressing the mess within to find clarity and order.

Job also realized that he needed to have a genuine conversation with God. To do this, Job had to quiet his mind. Many of us avoid quieting our minds because it requires us to listen rather than speak. This leads to a discussion on prayer; in the Western world, prayer is often a one-sided conversation. You see this in churches across America—it is taught that way. You pray, tell God your needs, give thanks, declare it done, and then get off your knees. Some even boast about how long they spend in prayer. But what has God said during your monologues? In Job's dialogues, God did most of the talking, which doesn't resemble the Western prayer approach. If you were seeking advice from a billionaire on achieving wealth, would you talk over them or listen intently?

We can navigate our lives with greater wisdom and alignment with our divine purpose by understanding and applying these lessons, as Job did.

Lastly, Job's transformation was marked by his renewed dialogue with God, wherein he realized he needed to quiet his mind to truly listen—a stark contrast to many modern practices of prayer, which often resemble monologues rather than dialogues. Like any meaningful conversation, true communication with the divine requires listening as much as, if not more than, speaking.

In closing, Job's journey teaches us about the inherent perfection within each of us as creations of God, the transformative power of self-reflection, and the profound impact of aligning our lives with divine principles. His story is less about the trials themselves and more about personal evolution, the renewal of faith, and the ultimate realization of one's inherent divine potential. As you reflect on Job's story, consider the challenges he faced and the profound spiritual awakening he achieved, reminding us that within every hardship lies the seed of equivalent or greater benefit.

9

WHAT HAPPENED TO ME

Now that you know what happened to Job, let me tell you how I came to myself. As I mentioned earlier, I had lost everything and moved in with my daughter, who was in her twenties. I came back feeling defeated and hopeless. I was so broke that I could spell the word broke with three extra zeros. I had no access to borrow money from banking sources, and my only source of banking was Cash Ap. Hell, I was so broke I couldn't even qualify for a payday loan. I also could no longer borrow from any of my family and friends because I either:

1. I had borrowed so many times they were exhausted to lend to me
2. Some of them I hadn't paid back, and I didn't have the money to currently
3. Others had their own life challenges they were dealing with
4. My personal pride would no longer allow me to

I picked up another contract assignment with a 2-week pay guarantee in which I had to give money to my daughter and use the rest to live off. While working, I searched for other assignments and even jobs, to no avail. When the money ran out, my mind went into despair. I started looking hard at my life through the wrong lenses. I looked at where I was living and how I was living. I focused on the failures that I had created along the way. I was hurt and confused because I knew who God was, or so I thought. I spent my days in spiritual practice, and I knew everything happened for a reason. But I couldn't personally understand why that was the reason and why these experiences had to happen. I found myself taking walks to where I needed to go, and I also spent a lot of time walking Bently. It was during those walks that I began to focus on Job. At first, I thought of how I could identify with him in his pain, but then God kept impressing me with what I already knew about the story. As I walked and thought throughout the days, Job became impressed upon me stronger and stronger until I knew that I would have to dive in and see what the Spirit was trying to tell me. I had a tiny skeleton of an idea of what this book would look like, but I knew the rest of the details would unfold as I wrote this book. But I also knew that before I could write this book, something in my life had to shift. I just couldn't figure out what.

Well, the shift came one day as I was at home thinking about Job, again. But this time, I was trying to focus on his conversation with God; although honestly, I hadn't even read the bible in years, I just knew some things. At that moment, I had to get quiet and really hear the inner god within. That quiet moment was the beginning of life, and it started to open again for me. I had first to acknowledge what I knew; my life was the sum of what I had been creating. I broke down in that acknowledgment. I'm so grateful that our loving Universal Spirit prevents us from staying there. God wanted me to take my focus off what was happening to me and focus on the lessons from those experiences. The lessons from those experiences didn't all hit me at once. Those lessons became realizations over time as I began writing this book.

One of the things that I realized is that there were times when I struggled with tremendous self-worth. A lot of that stemmed from my encounters with men in my early childhood. Times when I was not given the choice to decide if I wanted to say no to things. It made me take a hard look back on my relationships with men; how I was the pleaser in the relationship because deep down, I went with their choices in how they treated me. After all, a part of me felt like I couldn't say no. My power, in essence, was stripped from me sexually in early childhood. My decision to write erotica, in some ways, was a way to take my power back. I also learned how judgmental people can really be when writing erotica, especially those closest to you. But it also showed me that if my closest circle could judge me, it was highly probable that I had been extremely judgmental in situations. I became very aware. I also thought about my friendships that had all dissolved. Those people were satisfied when I saw myself as unworthy. I chose those people to play a part in my life to show me how little I valued myself. The more I saw value in myself, the more I realized it was ok to let those people leave.

I also learned in this process that I was the main person in my life that mattered. What I think about myself matters the most to me. It's quite alright to value the opinion of others.

But if it doesn't align with how you feel about yourself, and if it isn't coming from a place that aligns with the attributes of God, then it doesn't matter. But I also had to learn and be those attributes that God embodies every day. We know internally what those things are: be love, creative, intentional, giving and compassionate, be happy. Things like that are attributes that God embodies.

I thought about my financial ups and downs over the past five years. I thought about how I grew up watching my mom struggle financially, how we got evicted, how rent-to-own places stalked us after hours to get their belongings because she was behind on payments. I watched all our belongings being thrown on the curb while we were waiting for her boyfriend, who had promised to secure housing for us, only to find he had taken her money and left us homeless. I remember the five of us moving into my sister's two-bedroom flat apartment, already occupied by her, my niece, and her husband. One of the five was my autistic, non-verbal son Aaron, who was about five at the time. All those experiences and my own had shaped my thoughts about money and created a fear of possessing it. I realized that there was nothing wrong with having wealth. It is just a matter of where your heart truly is when you obtain those riches. Deep down inside, I feared losing it all, and I did. But I also learned that sometimes, some of us must be stripped of everything to get something greater. When I say everything, on this journey, I had to forget everything that I learned about life and God and find new information that would help me in my latter years.

God also wanted me to know that everything goes back to creation, and free will gives us the power to choose what we want to create. I had to look back at what I was creating.

Sure, I had manifested a lot of good things in my life that I wanted, but did those things make me happy? Some did. I focused on the good things I had created and accomplished. My life had been full already, and I had peace in that knowledge, but now I had to figure out what my life would look like in the future. I wanted to live fully because, through this process, I realized that God loves living through everything we create. Music, art, and writing are only small examples of how God enjoys living through us. When we love our children, God loves through us. When we travel and learn about different cultures, God enjoys the experience. When we travel, when we vacation, when we work, and when we love what we do, God loves it too. From this perspective, I decided to create my new life and asked God to give my soul new knowledge for my greater good along this journey. Again, all this realization did not come in one conversation with God. These things began to unfold as I started writing this book.

After my first internal conversation with God, when I got quiet, I received a full-time job offer from a life insurance agency with an hourly rate plus monthly bonuses. At the same time, a former co-worker was texting me repeatedly about a life insurance opportunity that was 100% commission. I ignored his messages over the next few weeks as I needed something stable. As the days approached to start my new job, I felt uneasy. I wanted to make money but didn't feel like this was the way. When I logged into my technical training set-up, and there were 250 others on the call, I felt like my belief was re-affirmed. On the day I was supposed to start, my stomach got queasy. I knew deep down that taking this job would not work for me. I couldn't see a financial end and thought, "I'll already be three weeks in the hole anyway.

Why not find something else?". I also thought I could hold out another three weeks for a contract assignment. After all, the company I was working with really liked me. At that moment, I received a text message from my former co-worker again. I called this man and told him he could shove his so-called opportunity where the sun didn't shine. I made that call, and he smiled through the whole conversation. He asked me just to be open to what he was offering. Of course, my guarded mind probed and asked a few questions, and then I agreed to watch a video he sent me. After watching the video, I knew that was the direction I was supposed to go. It was risky; there were no steady promises of a weekly income without working hard to learn their system. There were no promises of pipe dreams, just the guarantee that following their system and way of doing things would bring me a six-figure income.

I went with my gut and chose the opportunity over the job. My friends and family looked at me like I was insane. At the same time, the money was not immediately rolling in. I was grateful that I had income coming in to survive off of, but the people around me saw it as another flaky idea that I would move on from. So, not only did I have to contend with the thoughts and opinions of those close to me, but I also questioned if I could really do it and for how long. What I found, however, was that I kept showing up. Before you start your day, you can attend training and personal development sessions. I loved it! The work was mentally challenging, but the company balanced it with personal development designed to enhance your whole life. I dug into the process and discovered at the same time that I was changing my personal life and getting inspiration on how to enhance my business. I had to forget everything I knew about having a work ethic, about sales, and my perception of what it took to be an entrepreneur. So, not only was I getting a spiritual overhaul, but I was also in the school of life in the financial arena, so go figure. It was then time to start writing the book, which would involve splitting my time between selling life insurance and writing it. Not only that, but I also had to find a way to balance my work, family, and spiritual life. In the unfolding of this process, as I began writing the book, I knew I needed more of God, and I had to find out exactly what that meant. I also knew that writing this book would require some level of research, which came from the source of the topic, the bible. As I embarked on the journey of writing this book, God took me on a journey of my own, and as it unfolded, I saw the beauty in the journey every day.

10

AS MY LATTER UNFOLDS

A s my life unfolds and I finish this book, I can honestly say that the journey of life is becoming so beautiful. I didn't say that things still didn't happen to me; trials and challenges can and will come to all of us. But I learned in many ways how to manage the things that come to me in a way that aligns with God. And that's why this journey has been so beautiful.

The spiritual journey has been amazing. I remember asking my soul to give me what I needed to know for this leg of my journey, and it was in the middle of this journey I realized I was given what I had asked for. To understand the spiritual, I had to understand the physical. I always knew about the law of attraction and other spiritual laws in place, but God was trying to show me a bigger picture. I was familiar with Rhonda Byrnes, but then I began to really listen to her story. As I began to go into silence, I stumbled across information from famous doctors such as Joe Dispenza. Listening to his lectures helped me understand scientifically what happens to my body when I allow my life to be governed by the traumatic things that I focus on in life. That journey led me to people like Greg Braden and Billy Carsen and interviews hosted by Danika Patrick. I found myself in my own school of sorts, taking in all that God was showing me through all these people and more. I tuned into "The Power of Intention" by Wayne Dyer and listened to Bob Proctor's mindset-changing materials. When I came across materials from Shaman Durek, my life began to change, and things started to unfold for me even more. I opened myself up to beliefs that I knew were internally there, and I stopped questioning what I or anyone else believed.

I learned that God is way too big to put into words. I began to look at all of creation differently. I see lessons every day in creation and appreciate all things God created because they are beautiful. I also see in creation, everything has an unfolding period. A baby in the mother's womb takes a specific time to come into this world. The unfolding of a caterpillar to a butterfly has a specific time. An acorn becomes an oak tree over a different process of time. I also realize God is not in division, separation, hate, fear, or anxiety. We all come from the source of everything and are connected. In God, there is no black or white, there is no good or bad, and all the rules that we as humans have placed on what we should be and what God is has been destroying us. I also learned we are so much more than these bodies we live in. Our mind is a powerful tool that, if appropriately used the way God intended, can function in harmony in your life, contributing to a harmonious life in society.

I learned to be very mindful and aware of what I thought about, spoke about, and even allowed in my current environment. I learned scientifically that we are nothing but energy, so by mining my mind and thoughts, I am contributing to the positive stream of consciousness that makes this world a better place. When I focus on things God is not, I contribute to tearing down oneness. I also learned to be an expression of love by showing love to everyone around me. You would be surprised how far a smile and word of appreciation go in someone else's life. The attributes of God cost you nothing, so why not give them away? I have a new appreciation for music, nature, and human civilization, so much so that I find myself in beautiful tears and random giggles as I appreciate my life unfolding. I started meditating and going into silence every day and looking forward to it, wishing every day I had just a bit more time to spend with God before my day started. I began studying Quantum Physics. This may sound crazy to some of you, but I was hungry for what my soul needed. All this information I stumbled across was working because my friends and family noticed the changes in me. My daughter mentioned to me one day that while she was having a conversation with her best friend, she questioned why I was so damn happy. Of course, this made me burst into laughter. She told me that she could not physically see anything happening differently in my world, yet I was always smiling and singing.

I am watching the excitement of my physical latter unfolding as well. As I finish this book, I have been in the insurance industry for almost nine months. I have earned an all-expense paid trip for two to Costa Rica at the Four Seasons Hotel. I took one of my best friends on this trip with me to celebrate her birthday. I am also on track for a trip next year on a new luxury cruise liner called the Celebrity Beyond that will be sailing to the Bahamas, St. Thomas, and St. Croix. I have been on a couple of cruises, but not like this. This ship has luxury suites with butlers, and I am excited to be able to experience this with the people I work with.

Work is going well, and I have now begun saving for what I want to accomplish in the near term. I'm also on a short list of candidates they are looking for to promote, so we'll see how that unfolds. I went from having nothing to starting a savings account and having healthy savings. By the time this book is released, I'll have another audiobook released for my previous novel. The narrator is a beautiful soul who is excited about getting my work out there in audible form. God also brought back something big and amazing that I had forgotten about. In 2016, when I returned to Aetna, I connected with a former co-worker who had an idea for an invention she shared with me one day on one of our runs to the cafeteria. I got very excited for her and asked how I could help. She didn't have all the money to work with a company she found to get started, and I borrowed money from my 401K to help make it happen. Fast forward eight years later, she contacted me with the trademark and the marketing company for her amazing idea. We met with the marketing team, and as I write this book, that invention prototype is being created. This invention will be in households, restaurants, airports, and schools everywhere, generating millions of dollars for all our families. I won't disclose the name of the invention for NDA reasons as this book is being written, but I know this alone is a game changer for my life.

So, as you can see, the unfolding of my latter is far greater than everything I went through to get where I'm going. As a spiritual being, I realize that I am constantly growing, and I embrace who I am. I love to laugh and dance. I sing and make up fun songs in my head. I am totally ok with who I am, whatever that may be. Will I continue to write erotica? Probably. Because a couple of books still need to be written, and my podcast now has listeners in 62 countries. I also acknowledge that I am a very sensual being, and the things that happened to me early in life that caused sexual trauma were designed for me to feel helpless in my expression of my sexuality. I can be sensual and spiritual, too.

What else is next? I have no idea. But what I am excited about is living this life in a beautiful way and watching it unfold. I'm not afraid to make perceived mistakes because they serve as lessons I need along the way. I am grateful for every experience that I've had in life. From my marriage, I learned what being provided for felt like. Through my relationship with my young lover, I realized how it felt to have a mutual exchange of head-over-heels love, something I'd never experienced before. From all that I've accomplished and the friends and family I've obtained, I realized that my life is already full. I could go on and on, but I think you get the picture.

So, what does all this mean for you? What did you get out of this book? Only you can answer those questions. My assignment in this collective contribution was to write this book and pray that it gets into the hands of the reader who needs to read it. It may mean that if you go within, you can take a life of unhappiness, understand it, and transform it into whatever bliss you want your life to be. Was this book for me? Oh absolutely. I had to research it, get quiet, and most of all live it. It is humanly impossible to honestly write a book about God and not experience God in a life-changing way. My prayer is that even if one idea or concept opens you up and brings you closer to God, then I know that your life will change. Again, every idea and every concept need not be for you; take what resonates. I also know that I will never look at the book of Job the same or the things I go through the same. Our trials are not an extension of our unworthiness. We came into this world more than worthy. Trials are just things we experience as we navigate our greatness in this world we live in. The only limits we have are the ones we place on ourselves. And because I am aware of this, I know there is nothing I can experience in this physical world that can truly harm me because everyone and everything works together for my greater good, and I for its greater good. I know I live by the mantra that I learned that brings me peace and joy and embodies God and what I understand of creation. All is well, and everything is unfolding perfectly for me, for you, and for creation.

THE END

ABOUT THE AUTHOR

Jaylonna Stevette is a writer, speaker, mentor, entertainer, and entrepreneur who transitioned from a six-figure corporate America salary to guiding others in fulfilling their life's work. A spiritualist at heart, Jaylonna believes we possess the power within to dramatically change our circumstances. Described as smart, fierce, sexy, and in control, she is an executor who gets things done. Raised by a single mother of four, Jaylonna understands the challenges of single motherhood and the complexities of life in such circumstances.

Jaylonna's childhood was marked by experiences that deeply influenced her, with writing and entertainment as safe outlets for expression. Her stories, rooted in real-life themes, resonate with readers. Jaylonna's writing style is diverse, spanning various fiction genres to self-help and personal testimonials, showcasing her ability to tap into different streams of her artistic talent.

Her writing career began with assisting a local playwright in Columbus, Ohio. In 2012, Jaylonna wrote and produced her first stage play, "The Lounge," which sold out its first weekend and tackled the issue of domestic violence, captivating audiences. By 2014, "The Lounge" was featured at both the Atlanta Black Theater Festival and the DC Black Theater Festival.

Jaylonna has taken on multiple roles in the film industry, including extra, script supervisor, set location manager, and unit production manager with Awalkonwater Entertainment. She hosts the podcast "Naughty Tales," reaching audiences in 64 countries on platforms including Amazon Audible.

Jaylonna's writing often weaves a central message into captivating stories that engage readers on a deep emotional level. Her ability to connect with her audience is appreciated for its authenticity and relatability.

Overcoming extreme depression and emerging from a loveless marriage, Jaylonna lost seventy-five pounds through self-discovery. This transformation has empowered her to inspire women of all ages to live happily and embrace the best version of their lives. Her diverse experiences and transparency have enabled her to profoundly impact others on their paths to greatness.

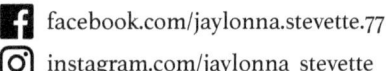

facebook.com/jaylonna.stevette.77

instagram.com/jaylonna_stevette

ALSO BY JAYLONNA STEVETTE

Getting Back 2 Happy: The Chronicles of Tabby

Almost Happy: The Chronicles of Tabby